TRUTH, LIES & HEARSAY

TRUTH, LIES & HEARSAY

A MEMOIR OF A MUSICAL LIFE IN AND OUT OF ROCK AND ROLL

JOHN SIMON

Dedicated to That Big Producer In The Sky

With Gratitude for giving me

Music

TRUTH, LIES and HEARSAY
A Memoir of a Musical Life in and out of Rock and Roll

CONTENTS

INTRO

Eastern Airlines Flight #4 from NYC's Idlewild airport nonstop to San Francisco.

I'm sitting for the first time in First Class, wearing my suit and Brooks Brothers shirt, my shoes shined, the only concession to what I think is my non-conformist nature being a loud necktie.

Across the aisle is my tripmate, Albert Grossman, music business powerhouse, manager of Bob Dylan and Peter, Paul & Mary, in his baggy jeans and suspenders over his ample belly, his gray hair pulled back in a free spirit pony tail and, in his rimless glasses and his 200 pound bulk, looking like a jumbo Benjamin Franklin.

He's comfortable up here in the front, joking with the stewardesses. I'm not exactly nervous but I feel like I'm heading off into newly-discovered virgin territory with a trusty guide.

That unexplored territory is Haight-Ashbury.

It's 1967 and the U.S. is on fire.

Riots, the war in Vietnam, protestors, cops, flowers stuck in the barrels of guns. A new word: Hippies.

But, from the safety of Manhattan, it's been like watching a movie. Hippies had been on the covers of magazines but this was before the Summer of

Love and the Be-In in Central Park. If there were hippies among us, they hadn't come out of their closet in force yet.

> In the years that immediately followed, I changed a lot. So much so that now, in all honesty, I can refer to myself as an "ex-Hippie."

But back then, though I considered myself a rebel in my way, I was part of the establishment. Up until a few months earlier I had been on a career track: an Ivy League education, rising up through a big corporation as a staff record producer—the good luck of the success of one record, "Red Rubber Ball", having catapulted me ahead several spaces on the Monopoly board of success to where I was now being charged with producing a hot San Francisco Band called Big Brother and The Holding Company featuring a singer who had become a poster child for the Flower Children of the Haight, Janis Joplin.

In the smallness of my world-view, I had no idea how my life would change once I hit The Haight. For one thing, that suit-and-tie disappeared into the dark depths of my closet. I would never be the same.

TRACK 1: MUSIC IS THE SOUP I SWIM IN.

'm a Compulsive Musician. Have been all my life. If I hear music, any music, my attention automatically goes to those notes and rhythms like a bear to honey. Can't help it. It's impossible to resist.

When my daughter brought the man who was to become her husband to introduce him to my wife and me, my attention was so magnetized by the music in the restaurant that I kept forgetting if his name was Jim or Joe. (Neither. It's Jeff.)

In addition to being compulsively musical, I'm real organized. I make lists. And those 2 qualities have paid off. I worked at a job where my musicianship and my stand-apart objectivity made me what later generations would call a good Project Manager.

I produced records for Janis Joplin, The Band, Blood-Sweat and Tears, Leonard Cohen, Simon and Garfunkel, Mama Cass and lots of others. You've heard of some of them. Probably.

But, in The Sixties, everybody had.

***

I never wanted to write this book.

But a few years ago a young man who had become a successful music manager took me under his wing and, among other things, said "Y'know, you ought to write a book."

I resisted. It seemed like a lot of work
And I imagined that potential readers of that book would be Diehard Rock and Roll Fans who would hope for one specific thing:

Dirt.

There were lots of other people who labored in the vineyards, cannabis plots and poppy fields of pop music who could recount hair-raising experiences hanging out with outrageous characters. Or else they THEMSELVES were real outrageous characters.

THEY could provide that dirt – not me.

There are lurid stories of producers doing vast amounts of psychedelics or taking LSD trips with their artists: tales of debauchery, crazy excesses and feats of unbelievable drug indulgences that some of those folks could relate first-hand.

I was a different animal, reluctant to jump into the fray with both feet. If I were to write a book, my rock experiences wouldn't hold a lava lamp to those stories.

After the session was over for the night, I went back to my life. It was my Day Job. Working with Janis Joplin and Big Brother was just going to the office for me.

I'm not equipped nor inclined to write that tell-all book.

And I wouldn't have the Objectivity of a professional rock critic either. No, I lived this journey myself.

So I couldn't write about it all in a historical context: about the Punks and the mosh pits of the 1980s nor the Teen Pop of the 90s. I was just an observer by then.

We each see ourselves in the center of our own real-life soap-opera. So anything I'd write would be seen through my own particular perspective as I bounced along through, among other places, the dizzy world of rock and roll.

Still I wondered:
Should I give it a shot? To write or not to write?
Do I have what it takes to do it?

Well, in high school, I joined the Writing Club and I wasn't kicked out. So if Miss Malinowsky considered me a writer, well, that's good enough for me.

Besides, I'm not afraid of hard work and it could turn out to be fun.

But then there's the question of memory and accuracy.

A lot of this stuff happened over 40 years ago. And, as my daughter, Sophie, said, people sometimes expect you to remember details from 40 years ago when they can't remember what they had for lunch!

I decided not to make things up. I owe that much to Diehard Rock Fans. But telling an entertaining story is like telling a joke well: sequence matters.

So although I remember lots of things from my years in and out of recording studios, in telling a tale I might re-order things a little bit.

And, after all, thankfully, writing a book about rock 'n roll is not a task that carries a lot of life-or-death responsibility with it. Telling these stories won't change the world. Compared to the Big Picture, pop music is small potatoes.

> In relation to Life As A Whole, pop music isn't like comparing apples and oranges. It's more like comparing a single apple to the entire apple output of the state of Washington between the years 1973 and 2004. (17 trillion 468 billion 364million, ten thousand seventeen apples.)

1 apple does not equal 17,468,364,010,017 apples.

> (That's a lie: I made up the number of apples in Washington. I'm not someone who looks gleefully forward to research.)

So whatever I write, in the Big Picture, won't really matter at all.

And be warned: I'm liable to express a perilous opinion or theory. I can be very critical at times.

> Coincidentally and sadly, I share the same name with an infamous theater critic, a particularly critical one.

A rubber stamp I had made.

"Do critics begin at the moment of birth
to separate good from inferior?
Do they say,' this is swell
but actually, well…
I preferred mommy's interior?'"

(from "In Defense of Critics", 1982)

(I wrote that lyric. And I should note here that any lyrics reproduced herein, unless otherwise indicated, are used with the kind permission of myself.)

I knew that Diehard Rock Fans would want answers to that question that will never die, "What was So-And-So <u>really</u> like?"

Well, I could lie and just make things up like:

- Leonard Cohen had considered a career as a cheese-maker.
  or
- Levon Helm spoke fluent Icelandic
  or
- Janis Joplin had a degree in lepidoptery

But you'd probably guess those things aren't true and, besides, if you're a big fan of any of those stars, you already know more than I do.

So I won't lie.

Although sometimes it's hard to know what's really true.

For instance, I read the following account in some publication that I had, in the past, credited as being creditable. I distinctly remember reading it cuz I couldn't have made up all the absurd details of this story.)

> Some commuters whizzing around the ramp onto the Long Island Expressway at six in the morning noticed a huge man, well over six feet tall and around 300 pounds, lying naked in the ditch.

> It turned out not to be a man, but a skinned gorilla.

> Apparently the simian corpse had fallen out of a truck negotiating the curve before dawn at a speed too fast to keep a skinned gorilla aboard on its way to—get this — a hot dog plant!

I didn't do a fact check because, whether or not it's true, it's a good story and everybody (if I'm a good example of "everybody") loves a good story.

> It made me wonder: how did he or she die? Old age? Murdered by the villainous corporate hotdog company that would try to convince us that he/she died a natural death—an accident? Slipped on a banana peel?—(a likely occurrence among gorillas perhaps).

But enough of that.

Chances are that's not why you started reading this book. But this is all leading somewhere.

Rock and Roll.
Truth, Lies or Hearsay.
Whichever.
Everybody loves a good story.

It's entertainment.

The Nairobi Trio. Famous Gorillas and a big influence on my youth.

For instance, here's a true story. It too has nothing to do with rock 'n roll. But it's a really cool story.

And I know that it's true.

TRACK 2: FOLKS' MUSIC

This happened when Libby, my mom, was in her twenties. She was still single and a "good looker".

She was visiting <u>her</u> mom, my grandmother, who had taken a summer job as the social director of a camp in the Adirondacks.
One weekend my dad arrived at the camp with a bunch of his pals.
One of them asked Libby out for a date in NYC for the following weekend. But my dad did an end run and asked her out for the Thursday night before that.

5 days later, after they'd met just that one time, he showed up at her door for that first date and asked, " Would you rather go see a movie or get married?"
My mother, a game gal if there ever was one, said, "I've seen a movie."

Right away, they drove down to Maryland where prenuptial blood tests weren't required and stayed married for 40 years.

Folks

TRACK 3: HIGH ON APPLE PIE

Looking back on the halcyon days of my youth, I sometimes recall it as The 25-cent Era. At an age when I was just learning how to count I noted that everything my parents bought cost 25 cents: a loaf of bread, a gallon of gas, a pack of cigarettes, a magazine.

Libby and Lou settled in Norwalk, Connecticut, an average town of average size with average people in an average era of postwar insecurity. America was proud, full of itself because we won the war. But unsure, with the threat of communism and a fragile peace.

> *"... I wasn't born in a Delta shack*
> *with the Appalachians at my back.*
> *I was born in a little New England town.*
> *The town was high on Apple pie,*
> *We marched along on the Fourth of July*
> *But in the sea of progress we got drowned.*
> *Biography of me..."*
>
> (from "Biography", 2002)

My dad had The Music Gene. He had played violin all his young life and had considered it as a profession. But, after graduating from NYU, he went to Juilliard and, as he told it, he heard kids who could play circles around him. So he decided that music would be his avocation. He took up a more secure profession. He became a doctor.

But that wasn't to be my future.
I wouldn't be making house calls.

Nor would I be sitting behind a desk.

Or selling widgets.

No normal job.

No, I would be working in the far-from-normal world of Rock and Roll.

There was always music in our house. Classical music mostly. My dad eventually started the Norwalk Symphony Orchestra. I inherited The Music Gene from him.

My sister, Barbara, got it too. Although she never studied an instrument, she has the uncanny ability to sing a perfect harmony part to any song she hears.

There was a popular board game called "Go To The Head Of the Class". For me, to quote Irving Berlin, "everything about it was appealing". Answer questions right and you move ahead. At my young age the goals of the game mirrored my own real-life classroom goals. I became an Achiever and soon found out that my achievements resulted in peer-respect and parental pride. In short, a Love Fest.

Plus, the name of the game itself appealed to me. It had a nice musical 6/8 ring to it: "GO-to-the-HEAD-of-the-CLASS."

It reinforced any inclination I had to be a Learner.

At age 4 I was introduced to a very small violin but the scratchy sounds I got out of it led my mom to lobby for a change-in-plans and I was switched to the piano where mistakes aren't quite as painful to listen to.

I had a piano teacher. But I never practiced enough. I had good enough ears and I was a good enough sight-reader so that some weeks I never practiced at all and showed up for my lesson sight-reading my assignment for only the 2nd time.

As I grew up I hardly ever practiced. I preferred being outside playing with my pals instead.

(Note suspenders. Must've been the style for kids in the Forties.)

Then one day I got it: all that tedious repetition of a particular difficult passage and suddenly I could play it easily. I must've been about seven and I hadn't felt that much pleasure since I was 3 and managed to count to 20, negotiating those difficult numbers that end with "-teen".

I used to hear my dad tune his violin. After learning to recognize the sound of those 4 violin strings, E, A, D and G, I found I had perfect pitch. And later I could write down the pitches of bird songs.

But many years later that became a handicap. Whenever asked to transpose music from one key to another, I'd see one note on the page and hear a different one with my ear. Disorienting. So I've had to work to <u>not</u> have perfect pitch!

The first music I remember liking came from recordings of Sousa marches. And the first music I remember liking even more than the Sousa marches was "Open The Door, Richard" by Louis Jordan.

(Many years have passed since some of the recordings that will get mentioned here were familiar to most pop music fans. But, thanks to the internet, if I refer to a song, you don't have to lay out a wad of cash to hear the entire album, as you would have back then. In most cases, if you want to listen and find out what I'm talking about, it's just a download click and pennies away.)

By the time I was a teenager, somehow the record of Benny Goodman's 1938 Carnegie Hall Jazz concert found its way to a spot in my dad's collection of classical music: a raucous intruder in the realm of Mozart, Beethoven, and Tchaikovsky.
I liked it.

Then a sampler that Columbia Records issued called "I Like Jazz" joined the Goodman concert and soon I had a subscription to the Jazztone society and a new record each month. I heard Erroll Garner, Art Tatum and lots more. Then my mom brought home a 10 inch LP from the supermarket, a jazz sampler that RCA put out. It was part of a series. The one I had was Volume 10, the letters O through R. So I heard Kid Ory, Charlie Parker, Oscar Peterson, and Django Reinhardt.

Meanwhile I begged my dad for a piano teacher who could teach me something other than the Bach inventions and Mozart and Beethoven piano sonatas I was learning. And that teacher was Ande Wuhrer who had once played on the road with several Latin bands.
Ande taught me how to play boogie-woogie and stride piano. He taught me about chords and lead sheets and improvising.

A high school classmate, Eddie Maestro, had put together a band of high schoolers that he called "The Blue Knights." Eddie was good at getting us gigs at ethnic weddings. So we played our share of Italian, Hungarian, Polish, and German festivities.

l-r: Dave Poe, BobHodge, Pete Waldeck,
Alan Ferguson, me, Eddie Maestro

Later, along with my pal Dave Poe, a really fine musician, I left Eddie's Blue Knights and we formed another band which we named "The Group". (Funny that I should eventually work with another act with a similar generic name: "The Band".)

Another time I had a quartet and I'd heard of a character named Simon Legree in a book I'd never read, Uncle Tom's Cabin, so, I considered the euphonious name, "John Simon and The Legree Three". But then , when I learned that Simon Legree was a very very very Bad Dude indeed, I realized that was a terrible idea.

I'll never forget the day when we tyro jazz-ers suddenly grokked improvisation. A few of us were jamming at my house and I remember Joe Scire, our tenor player, lying on his back on our couch and playing through the chords of "Perdido" in ecstasy.

Which reminds me of another tenor sax story. (And for those of you who have been patiently waiting, here's a rock and roll story – finally!)

Jimmy Seals and Dash Crofts, known professionally as Seals and Crofts, had formerly been members of a band called The Champs who had a huge hit (later popularized by Pee-wee Herman) called "Tequila". Jimmy played the tenor in that band.

Because it was such a huge hit, they were on the road playing one-nighters in town after town, often arriving barely in time for the show.

Like several odd bands of that period that wanted to add a little something extra to their show, The Champs included acrobatics in their act. Jimmy Seals, playing his sax at the time, would walk to the edge of the stage for his solo and do a flip, and then swagger up the aisle blowing away.

He told me that one time he did his flip and didn't realize that there was an orchestra pit. When he came to his senses, fans were leaning into the pit and applauding.

The other story they told me was that Dash, the Champs' drummer at the time, was one of those drummers who tied all of his drums together with a rope so that they wouldn't slide all over the stage and the rope was tied to his drum stool. Often they'd arrive just in time to perform and find Dash's drums all set up and ready to go. Only, one time, his drums had been set up with the bass drum spikes accidentally stuck in the chain that weighed down the stage curtain. So, when the curtain went up, the drums went up and the drummer with them.

***

We fledgling jazz musicians looked down on rock 'n roll. It was just too easy. Many of the songs consisted of a chord pattern you could call One-Six–Two-Five, referring to the notes of the scale. That is, in the key of C for instance, the bass notes would be C to A to D to G.

Those were the simple chords of "Heart and Soul" for goodness sake, the first song that 9 out of 10 pre-adolescents played to show-off on the piano.

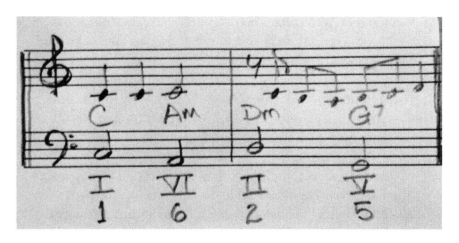

We Jazz Tenderfoots were in the thrall of some kind of adolescent snobbery. Those of us who could actually read music were so proud of our ability to read chord symbols like C#m7 (b5). I mean, THAT was Jazz.

Just a few years ago I looked back at our high school yearbook and was amazed at how many ordinary teenagers back then listed jazz as their favorite music.
Where did all those jazz fans go?

The first rock 'n roll song I ever played? "Shake Rattle and Roll".
I went with Dave Poe to far-off, exotic Bridgeport and we bought
the sheet music in a music store.

We also ventured even farther—New York City by train, where we
bought a Webcor tape recorder which we lugged back to Norwalk. It's
pre-transistor weight felt like 300 pounds and probably was.

We learned songs from these little song collection books called
"Combo Orks". They were made for kids just like us. Each was
issued by a music publishing house and contained solely songs
from their catalogue.

But what we really pined for and drooled over were … The Fake Books!
These books had over 1000 songs, unlimited by the publisher's right to
print them and, hence, completely illegal.

(if you can imagine that, long before the current climate of the
everything-for-free internet.)

These were as unattainable as The Holy Grail for youngsters like us. They
were suited for Pros because, unlike regular sheet music, each song had

only its melody and chord names. From those chord names alone you had to know how to transform the letters into actual chords that sounded good.

It wasn't until after college when I arrived in NYC that I managed to purchase my own illegal fakebook. It was like a drug buy! I actually had to meet this shady guy in a trenchcoat on the street who, looking left then right, opened up a large black suitcase and handed me volumes 1 and 2 for thirty bucks apiece. Then he was gone in a flash.

Those 2 books continue to serve me well fifty years later.

When I was 15 I had a summer to kill because I didn't have my driver's license yet so it was decided that I would go to The New England Music Camp in Maine which sounded like fun.

I liked the camp part of it: swimming, baseball, hikes, girls. But the music part was harder. I had individual piano lessons from a Teutonic task-mistress named Lisl Braun who gave me an inkling of how much you REALLY have to practice to get REALLY good.

I got kicked out—not for any musical reason, but because one night I passed a cabin with a blackboard on which the questions for an exam the next day had been written.

It was a fill-in-the-blanks quiz.

Uh-oh. Temptation. Trouble.

I filled in the blanks with every dirty word a 15-year-old wiseass would know.

Like:

"The wind instruments consist of the <u>vagina</u> and <u>penis</u> families."

"The indication, "Vivace" means <u>Fuck you</u>."

Etc.

To 15-year olds, this is The Stuff Of Genius.

Kicked out!
And I'd had a upcoming date for The Big Dance with the daughter of the Music Camp's director, the cutest cupcake in the camp.

    "How could you?!", she pouted.
    "How could I <u>not</u>", I replied.

Looking back, I see what aspects of my personality my misdeed revealed:
    Creativity.
    The ability to amuse my peers.
    Oblivious disregard for any unpleasant consequence.

TRACK 4: GOING PRO

My mom was no great cook. A disproportionate number of our meals came out of cans. So it was always with anticipation bordering on hysterical delight when my sister and I were told that we were going out for dinner.

A favorite destination was DeAngelo's Steakhouse where I would invariably order spaghetti. (Back then, unless you were Italian you never heard the word "pasta".)

But in all our Sunday dinner pilgrimages to this land of sugar-y tomato sauce, we had never noticed the door to a back room, nor the stream of men going through it.

My first Real Professional Job, apart from the Blue Knights, was in that back room.

I was 15 and hired as the piano player with a bunch of seasoned, <u>grown-up</u> musicians.

> Hugh Golden was a local music contractor and someone my dad knew. So when Hugh offered to hire me for a professional job, my dad must've figured it'd be good for the kid to get some professional experience.
> Little did he know.

In that back room of DeAngelo's Steakhouse our repertoire consisted of songs like "Night Train", "Harlem Nocturne" and the like. If you're a musician, you know where this is going: we were backing a stripper.

She did a towel dance. Here is a schematic showing the location of the various elements in the performance.

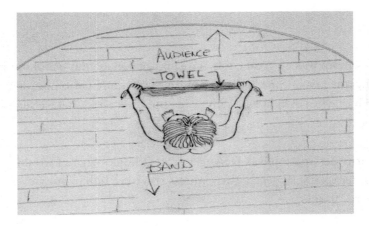

The stripper was skillful at keeping the towel between herself and the audience but the band was upstage of her and had a real good view of the goings-on (and the comings-off).

And in a flash I realized that there was more to life as a professional musician than my piano teacher had led me to believe!

> Incidentally I will never get "upstage" and "downstage" confused because of a story that Bill Roos, our junior high school band director, told.
> It seems that when he was in the army, he gave a clarinet recital accompanied by another soldier on a pump organ behind him.
> Like many very old stages, this one was raked, slanted toward the audience. So, as his accompanist pedaled, the organ inched its way downstage and Bill had to hold it in place with his foot.

There it is. Upstage. Downstage.

I also had a Brush With Greatness at the DeAngelo's Steakhouse job. I found out that the drummer (a vital element in any stripper's routine) had previously been Horace Silver's drummer before Horace, also a Norwalk native, had left town for the big time. Horace had been one of my idols. I was so proud of him and of Norwalk for spawning such a wonderful jazz musician.

It gave me hope.

TRACK 5 – P. U.

So I'm walking down the crowded, pimply adolescent halls of Norwalk High between classes when a kid I knew only slightly approached.

"Hey. I'm Jim Shearwood. School's boring so I'm thinking we could all put on a show. Y'know sort of like a Judy Garland / Mickey Rooney musical. I wonder if you could help me pick some songs to do."

I thought, "What the hell. Why not?" But I wanted to write original songs instead. Basically because writing them myself seemed easier to me than doing the research.

We wrote two original musicals, one a review and one a book show. They were the first songs I'd written since the marching song I wrote for my cub scout den when I was 10 years old.

I bought a book to help me write lyrics, The Clement Wood Rhyming Dictionary. I still have it. At first I felt dizzily empowered by it's long lists of rhymes and I wrote terrible lyrics like:

"I can't give you a palace
Or a silver chalice.
Or an aardvark or the Zuyder Zee."

Since the casts of our shows were made up of students, we played to packed houses of parents and friends, and that achievement was instrumental ('scuse the pun) in getting me into Princeton University.

Of course the fact that my mother's second cousin was a Princeton music professor helped too.

So there I was in the fall of 1959 showing up in Princeton, New Jersey at a serious-institution-of-learning, a different arena than Norwalk High School which, like so many other American high schools of the time, could have been a model for "Grease".

Sure, I had written a couple of high school musicals but everyone else at P.U. was at least a valedictorian, a yearbook editor, a football star, or had built a functioning rocket ship.
And to top it off, over half of them were "preppies": they'd come from private schools where (and this was a shocker) teachers were their <u>friends</u>! At N.H.S., teachers were The Enemy.

Thinking at first that life at college would be as leisurely as high school, I signed up for every musical activity available: I was in the band for football games, I accompanied the glee club, I tried out for all the singing groups, I wrote jazz arrangements and played in the Big Band (led by my pal, drummer Phil Weinstein, who shall figure in this story when we get to The Band's second album) and I played for dances at other colleges.

Then one day I saw an announcement in the Daily Princetonian inviting college bands to submit audition tapes for the First Georgetown University Intercollegiate Jazz Festival.
On a lark, I called other musicians on campus to see who might be free the next day to make a tape. A bass player, drummer, trumpet player, tenor player and two trombonists said to count them in. So that night I wrote some arrangements for this unorthodox combo and we made a tape. Imagine my surprise when I found out that our band-which-wasn't-really-a-band had been chosen as one of six finalists in the competition.

So one weekend in the Spring we set off in a couple of cars for Georgetown University in Washington, D.C..

The judges for the concert were the immensely popular Dave Brubeck and Paul Desmond. We opened the show. We didn't win of course but, for some small comfort, neither did Chuck Mangione's band (Chuck later had a lot of commercial success).

> The winners were the Charles Bell Contemporary Jazz Quartet from Carnegie Tech and the runner-up was the North Texas State Lab Band, from a jazz program in which, if you lagged behind, you were tied to a longhorn steer and dragged from Lubbock to San Antone.

But, of all the musical activities on campus, the one that was the newest to me and also struck me as having the most potential was the Triangle Club, which, like our Mickey-and-Judy operation in high school, put together an original musical every year. But, unlike that ad hoc high school enterprise, the Triangle Shows had a long tradition which included a tour throughout the country during Christmas break. Past alumni of the Triangle Club included Jimmy Stewart, José Ferrer and fucking F. fucking Scott fucking Fitzgerald for chrisake.

> (I suppose the most notable Triangle alumna after I graduated was Brooke Shields. And by "notable" I mean one who some-times shows up on the covers of tabloids in supermarkets and sells make-up.)

So I dropped every activity except for the Triangle Club and wrote three original shows, went on four show tours.

> My God. The tales of Triangle would fill a book the size of this one.
> The creative side of Triangle was a lot of fun and sort of what I had expected it to be but the Social Side was something else.

The tours! I mention them here because it was my first experience of Going On The road.

But this wasn't an ordinary "Going On The Road."

Because we toured during Christmas Recess it had become the practice for the local Princeton Alumni Clubs in each town we visited to offer us up as convenient "stag lines" for the Debutante Balls that went on during that season.

We travelled by train in special Pullman cars and, for instance, our train would pull into Cleveland and the alumni at the local Princeton Club would get us rotten drunk at a cocktail party. Then we'd pull it together enough to do our show and afterwards put on penguin suits—white tie and tails—in order to masquerade as a proper stag line and head for the debutante ball at the Grand Cotillion Ballroom of The Sheraton Hilton.

The parents of the Debs imagined that we would be a proper set of young Ivy League gentlemen eager to flatter and fawn over a bunch of teenage girls who were distressingly overdressed. It was assumed that we would courteously squire their virginal maidens for a dance or 2.

They couldn't have been more wrong!
We were there to raise hell!

As we were we're funneled through the Receiving Line of Debs who were maintaining their gracious, upper-crust composure, we'd whisper risque innuendos to them. They'd blush like tomatoes and we'd head for the champagne table.

There would be an orchestra hired because the lack-luster stuff they played was the musical equivalent of cardboard-colored cardboard.

When the orchestra took a break, we'd leap to the bandstand and start trying to shake things up with some rowdier sounds.

Chased by other fellows in penguin suits (actual local boyfriends and brothers of the aforementioned virginal maidens), we would escape to our Pullman cars, pour ourselves into our bunks and wake up the next day to repeat our bad behavior in Louisville.

Sound like fun? You bet it was.

Speaking of drunks, I got an actual musical tip from a Triangle alumnus who had had great success writing jingles for the advertising industry, and who had come to hear what we'd written for our upcoming show that year.

He was, as alluded to, drunk but he pointed out something to me that I've kept in mind in relation to all the songwriting that I've done since and in the counsel I've offered to other songwriters.

> I had written a song on the piano that sounded fine on the piano but didn't quite work when it was sung. And he said, "Always <u>sing</u> any melody that's intended to be sung as you're writing it." Or , rather, he said, "Alwaysh shing any melody that'sh intended to be shung ash you're writing it."

TRACK 6 – TWO MILTONS

Milt Lyon and Milton Babbitt.
Milt Lyon was the professional director of the Triangle shows. He was brilliant and had great theater-sense. He had been a stage and TV director and for the previous 15 years he had corralled a bunch of crazy undergraduates and coaxed and coached them into assembling a passable evening of musical theater.

> One year we students wrote a show based on the premise that Queen Elizabeth wrote Shakespeare's plays. Messing with history as much as possible, I wrote a musical version of Macbeth – but with a happy ending!

Milt even improved my piano playing. He showed me how to play long notes with the thumb of my right hand as a sort of cello to glue a piano accompaniment together.

Milt was also the "responsible adult" for those hell-raising tours and, bless his soul, he was extremely permissive with us ("Boys will be boys.")
The only time I remember him exercising any control was when a trumpet player from our pit band got a little tipsy in a Pittsburgh hotel and decided he was a competent ledge-walker. That was hairy but Milt got him back inside

Milt Lyon

That was the same year Triangle's train crossed the country to play California for the first time and that same trumpet player got off the train during a Las Vegas refueling stop and never got back on.

He may still be there.

Because I was into so many musical activities instead of devoting time to study for my classes, I figured I had to either cut back on those things or sign up for the easiest major possible. The choice of a major was easy: music.

Milton Babbitt was the most remarkable teacher I ever met. A brilliant but personable guy with a basso speaking voice, small and wiry, bespectacled and intense, warm and laconic, the man could speak in perfectly organized paragraphs without once pausing to utter an "uh" or an "um".

He had a great sense of humor too. He once programmed a concert featuring the music of composers Benjamin Fine and Vincent D'Indy (pronounced "dandy") just so he could bill it as "Fine and D'Indy".

Milton Babbitt

He had been a full professor of mathematics but, when many in the music faculty got drafted one year, he filled the gap and became a professor of music.

As a composer he was one of the forerunners of serial music, in which notes were chosen for their mathematical relationships with each other rather than whether or not they simply sounded good. He often worked on the IBM computer that had been installed up at Columbia University. That early computer filled an entire classroom because its guts were full of tubes. This was the grandpappy of today's microchips that you can fit under your fingernail.

Babbitt on the IBM computer

But what Babbitt taught us was three centuries older than that. For three years we worked exclusively out of the Bach chorale books. We would be given a melody, most often an ancient one that had evolved through monks and folksong, and we were assigned to harmonize it.

In the course of this instruction, it became obvious to us that, with only 12 notes available in the scale of Western music, some harmonizations are better than others and, therefore, one way isn't necessarily as good as the next. There _is_ a best way.

Johann Sebastian Bach did it the best way.

A Bach harmonization of a familiar tune,
Martin Luther's "A Mighty Fortress Is Our God".

Milton Babbitt's mind was hardly limited to the 18th century. He was curious about all new music. It was rumored that he went into New York City to sit in with Ornette Coleman and see what that was about.

Hearsay.
But I believe it.

***

I graduated in 1963. Things were different then. In the last weeks of your senior year, job recruiters actually came to campus with offers of employment.

I had two job offers: one was to write copy for Anacin commercials for the Ted Bates advertising company in Chicago. The other sounded more vague: to be a trainee in New York City at Columbia Records.

They each paid $85 a week. The choice was easy.

If I had taken the advertising offer, this book would be about aspirin.

TRACK 7 — MEAT ON A STICK

had married between my junior and senior years when Nina and I were both merely 20. We got along fine and were courageously facing the world of grown-ups.

The day after I graduated, I was plopped into the Real World of New York City—a married man, a householder, an employee of Columbia Records. I had responsibilities.

Shocker!

I looked around at the hordes of people rushing around at a pace far faster than the casual amble of college students and thought, "My God! It's like a massive ANT COLONY ON DOUBLE ESPRESSOS !"

So I swallowed hard and realized that now I was about to plunge into NYC and become an ant myself.

Wasn't the Big Apple full of surprises!

My first day on the job at Columbia Records. My dream job? Maybe so. I was going to be an A & R man.

I knew what that was. It was the behind-the-scenes guy who directed the recording of a recording.

I went to the address for Columbia Records and reported to my training supervisor. He put together a program for me in which I would visit every aspect of the record business: from putting little pieces of vinyl into this waffle-iron gizmo at the pressing plant in Bridgeport to putting little pieces of green paper in the hands of radio station programmers and DJs.

Yes, the word is payola.

My first day on the job. A morning briefing session, and then ...

Lunch!

What do I do now? It hadn't occurred to me that Lunch was an important element in the work-force's day.

What to do? Others were leaving the building in pairs and groups to grab some food in a favorite joint. But I was on my own.

I walked out the door of 799 7th Avenue on a clear day in early summer and took in the neighborhood: Broadway, a few blocks north of Times Square. In some respects, the center of the world.
And, yes, I was getting hungry. I didn't want to sit down all by myself looking like a pathetic, lonesome soul who couldn't even get a lunch-mate – which I was.
So I decided to try one of the food joints where I could eat standing up, or maybe stroll with my chow.

And there it was: Meat On A Stick.

I had never seen anything like it. I couldn't identify the animal this meat came from. The taste was somewhere in the baloney area. It was as thick as my thigh but a perfectly-shaped cone and the animal must've been boneless because, except for a 3 foot long metal spike through this meat, there was no bone holding it together.

I pictured a herd of baloneys, easy prey for the baloney hunters because, being boneless, they just fell down a lot.

I came to find out that this exotic NYC delicacy was called a gyro, of Middle Eastern origin and sometimes pronounced close to "hero".

Those first fruits of my savoir-faire as a New Yorker didn't exactly excite my palette so I resolved, until the day when I would fall in with a jolly, cordial lunch crowd, to bring my lunch to work and eat at my desk.

But I didn't have a desk... Yet.

TRACK 8 – 799

7 99 7th Ave. was an ancient building. I worked there for two years before "Corporate" moved our homey operation to "Black Rock". During that time, I was shuffled around to seven different offices. Impressionable as this recent college grad was, I remember each of the floors and what went on there.

(But I also remember the names of all my elementary school teachers—I suppose I should clear them out of my memory-file to make room for some useful information.)

- The first floor at 799 7th Ave. was the Oh-Ho-So Chinese restaurant whose bar was the default meeting place for out-of-office conferences.
- The second-floor was the home of the A&R department, divided in two by a thick wall to separate the pop and classical producers from eating each other.
- The third floor was the domain of the art department.
- The fourth floor was sales, publicity, promotion.
- The fifth floor contained the editing, mixing and mastering rooms.
- And on the sixth floor were Studio A and Studio D.

799 Seventh Ave.

In this photo from the internet, someone has helpfully circled the structure added on top of the roof that housed the venerable Studio A, which would become a very important room in my life.

When you entered the trainee program at Columbia records, it was understood that you had to have a destination in the company after your training was complete. My destination was to be the Special Projects department.

Special Projects was the favored child of Goddard Lieberson, the erudite, suave, debonair, dignified, creative president of Columbia Records.

He was a legend then as he is now. Underling that I was, Goddard Lieberson was only a little bit more accessible to me than was the President of the United States. But, in the halls and studios of Columbia, I saw him and his aura enough to respect him as our Peerless Leader. After all, he had been born in England and was married to Vera Zorina, famous ballerina who had been in the movies and had excellent posture.

I remember Goddard coming out of his office after a meeting with someone and incredulously saying, "That man actually wore brown shoes with a blue suit!"

Bruce Lundvall, who was then in Columbia's sales department and of whom much admiring prose will be written later, told me this story:

> It happened at one of Columbia's wild annual sales conventions (always held in one of the hottest places on the planet in the middle of the summer, for reasons of economy). As Goddard was leaving an event in his limousine, an attractive hooker tapped on his window to get him to roll it down.
>
> In a voice like melting jelly, she confided in him, "I give the best blow jobs in Miami."
>
> Goddard with deep sincerity replied, "I'll bet you've made your parents very proud, my dear", rolled up the window and moved on.

Anyway, I was assigned to "Special Projects" which was Goddard's baby. Included under its rubric were the Original Cast recordings of Broadway shows, along with the "Legacy" recordings: thematically-focused coffee table packages including a book as well as a record, such as "The Confederacy", "The Union", "Mexico", "Badmen" and "The Irish Rebellion".

> There were others that were never finished, for one reason or another, like "Doctors, Drugs and Diseases".

So I was the new guy, fresh meat, to do all the grunt work on those projects.

And I learned.

While in the studio recording songs about doctors, drugs, diseases and badmen, I got my feet wet with simple recordings in which the engineer did all the work and I tried to absorb as much studio know-how as I could.
We recorded Ramblin' Jack Elliott, Sonny Terry and Brownie McGee, the Clancy Brothers and other folk-ish performers. It was very relaxed.

I was real lucky in that I drew a great boss: Charlie Burr. Charlie was a real upbeat, beaten down, somewhat dissipated, funny and intelligent guy prone to liquid lunches down at the O-Ho-So.

It was he alone in our department who had access to Lieberson. And he would dole out assignments to me or to any one of the freelancers who came in from time to time to help with a particular project.

Just looking at this photo that I found reminds me of how much I liked him.

The Original Cast albums were not as relaxed as the Legacy projects. Recording one of them was a much more expensive extravaganza so the details had to be worked out very, very carefully.

> In preparation for the recording of those Broadway show albums, I was sent to Boston, Philadelphia or Detroit with a stopwatch to time the songs in the show before the show opened on Broadway. That information would be printed right away on the album jackets which were manufactured weeks before the recording session. Then, after that session, the fresh-pressed vinyl would be slipped into them.

The recording itself was done at Columbia's magnificent 30th St. studio, a cavernous space that had been a church and could accommodate a huge symphony orchestra.

> (It was also the room transcendent pianist Glenn Gould chose to record his solo performances – wearing an overcoat and gloves with the fingertips cut off because he liked it cold—and also the room I later used for the first Moog synthesizer sessions we did with Simon and Garfunkel.)

"30th Street"   Glenn Gould trying out pianos

The cast albums were done on a Sunday, when there was no Broadway performance scheduled. The sequence in which the numbers were recorded was logistically logical: the orchestra's overture was recorded in the morning. Then the entire cast came in for the big numbers and eventually the duets and solos were recorded after the sun went down.

As each number was completed, Goddard and the authors would mark up the musical score and hand the tapes off to me or to my superior, Teo Macero, the colorful producer of Miles Davis and other jazz artists, and we would splice together the complete takes prior to mixing.

Then, after everyone else went home to sleep, Teo and I would take the tapes uptown to the mixing rooms and, with mixing engineers, he would mix the stereo of one side of the album while I mixed the monaural of the other. Then we'd switch and, at about four in the morning, go home and get some sleep ourselves.

When Goddard got in early in the morning, he'd give a listen to what we'd done and ask for a few corrections which we would then do and the tapes would be whisked off to the pressing plant in Bridgeport to be slipped into those waiting jackets and be in the Colony Records music store on Tuesday morning.

> In subsequent years, when faceless corporations with their production timetables took over record companies, the ability of independent record companies to turn on a dime was lost. The recording of a project now would have to be completed often six months before its release date. Christmas albums recorded in June!

I could only think back to those Tuesday morning Original Cast releases and shake my head.

TRACK 9 — A DAY TO REMEMBER

Florette Zuelke was maybe 10 years older than me. She joined us as a freelance in the Legacy department under Charlie Burr. She had a gap-toothed smile as wide as her home state of Wisconsin and was just a delight to be around.

One day she took me aside and asked me to be her chaperone for lunch. It seems she had been invited out by Harold Arlen, legendary composer of, among so many great songs, "Over The Rainbow". She felt she needed me there because Harold had "an eye for the women".
I didn't particularly relish the role she planned for me but I was really excited to be able to meet Harold Arlen, whose songs I loved.

And there he was: nattily dressed, wearing a carnation and looking out at the world through glasses with blue lenses.

> I can't imagine he was overjoyed to see me along for the ride but nevertheless he led us into an upscale restaurant a block away, The House Of Chan.

The restaurant was not very crowded and we had a very pleasant meal peppered by his showbiz stories.

I remember now in retrospect how polite, formal and unexpressive the Chinese waiters were.
I say "in retrospect" cuz, when we went outside it was like the earth had been struck by a meteor.

People were staggering on wobbly legs as if there was little gravity and they'd lost their bearings, sobbing hysterically and clutching each other. In a matter of seconds we found out why—Kennedy had been shot.

If you were a grown-up in 1963, you remember where you were that day. If you're not that old, well, people have written about that era. The sparkling, noble and joyous metaphor of Camelot had been in the air. We thought JFK's election would bring that kind of Shangri-la to America. He was the embodiment of "our" generation.

His predecessor, Dwight Eisenhower, "Ike", the hero of World War II was the embodiment of American quiet power. Ike wore a fedora, like the archetypical Fifties dad. He played golf, like that dad. He was the paterfamilias whose household authority was not to be questioned. He was married to an alcoholic frump.

He reminded me of my own dad (except for the alcoholic frump part.)

And here came the Kennedys. No fedoras. Golf replaced by sailing and touch football, more youthful activities. Not the authoritative father-figure, but the dashing older brother with a beautiful wife by his side.

His oratory was full of promise. Ike had been diffident, retiring. JFK was outgoing, loved, challenging the cob-webbed protocols of our parents, just as I challenged mine.

Then one awful day in Dallas he was killed.

And with JFK's death Camelot collapsed. That youthful invigoration that I had felt was drained from my heart and soul and I wondered if it would ever return again.

TRACK 10 – SALVATION AND BEYOND

Meanwhile there I was, learning my trade in the Special Projects department. But soon a problem came up. Columbia Records was suddenly "organized" when its owner, Corporate CBS, realized that this little record company was making money. On their corporate organization chart, it was decided that Special Projects had to be a division of either Pop music A&R or "Masterworks", the classical music section. Where would they put us?

To my horror Special Projects was classified as classical.

> This was extremely bad news for me. Musically-inclined as I was, my interests were not in classical music. Nor was my knowledge. As a graduating music major at Princeton I was required to take a needle-drop test which consisted of, as the name implies, a needle dropped at random in the middle of a classical recording with the test-taker asking you to "name that tune".
> Out of 35 examples I only got 3 right!

This was not a promising batting average if I hoped to join experienced classical music producers like John McClure, Tom Frost, Paul Myers and Tom Shepard who knew every classical piece of music ever written, every artist who ever recorded that piece and the names of their former spouses and pets.

Woe was me!

But deliverance came in the person of Ken Glancy.

Ken had just taken over as the head of A&R and was reviewing his staff. He called me into his office and said, "You don't belong in Masterworks. You belong in the pop department."

Hosanna!

I left my colleagues in languid Special Projects and moved into the jet-stream, clown car world of pop music.

So there I was, a pop record producer.

In those days producers never got credit on albums. So they really were unsung heroes. To make up for lost time I will sing some of their praises now.

Teo Macero, mentioned earlier, was Columbia's resident jazz producer. A snappy dresser whose internal speedometer was always a little bit above the legal speed limit, he made albums with Miles Davis, Charles Mingus, et al. The only other producer with a comparable number of jazz albums on Columbia was the venerable George Avakian. But George was a freelance.

John Hammond. John was the Dean of them all. The story of his life has been written about elsewhere. Coming from a distinguished and moneyed family, he was instrumental in the careers of Count Basie and Benny Goodman. With the young Goddard Lieberson, he had produced a famous blues concert at Carnegie Hall. He discovered Billie Holiday and Bessie Smith. He discovered Bob Dylan.
He came into work every day with his folded up newspaper and a cheerful attitude and had the respect of all.

Teo with Miles   John with Aretha   Tom with Dylan

Tom Wilson, an effervescent 6-foot-2 Harvard grad. He produced a variety of acts, including adding a rock rhythm section to Simon and Garfunkel's "Sounds Of Silence" thus saving them from obscurity and launching them on their careers. This overdub was done without their knowledge and they later discovered that they had a big hit.
Tom told me some record business tales like this one:

> One of his former mentors was a doo-wop producer. He wrote down all the doo-wop background nonsense syllables he used, like "shebang, shebang" or "whoop-whoop and kept them filed alphabetically in a little box to make sure he didn't use them again.

Mike Berniker was only a couple of years older than I was. He had come from Bucknell where he had been pals with Bruce Lundvall. Mike was one of those guys who sucked up all the air in the room. But it was an entertaining suck job. He was funny and full of himself and made fun of how full of himself he was. He had a few gold records on his wall that came from an artist he developed named Barbara Streisand.

Berniker with engineer, Frank Laico   Bob Johnston

Bob Johnston arrived after I'd been at Columbia for two years. You could tell he was a Southerner alright. He was also a songwriter or his wife was, or something about Elvis Presley was associated with him in some way. I think maybe he and his wife wrote some songs for an Elvis movie. Maybe it was "Dragstrip Cajun Moonlight Jailhouse Hoedown In Vegas".
Hearsay.

Whenever a new artist was signed, producers had to talk to the legal department about contracts and there were three lawyers: Mort Drosnes, Walter Yetnikoff and future music-business big cheese, Clive Davis.
Of the three, my favorite was Mort. The other two seem to have little time for me as a kid of little consequence, their minds perhaps leaping forward to the time when they'd each be the president of Columbia Records.

Clive   Bruce

night and day

Another future president of Columbia Records and a wonderful guy was Bruce Lundvall. While I was at Columbia, Bruce was in the sales department, a beehive of activity. Phones ringing, papers flying, people running around. It seemed like one of those stop-the-presses newspaper offices from the movies.

It was because of Bruce that I met Elizabeth Taylor and Richard Burton.

Because of their amorous realignments, these 2 movie stars were on the covers of every super-market checkout–line tabloid during a certain period in America's Pop History. When I was starting out at Columbia, Burton was doing Hamlet on Broadway and Goddard Lieberson wanted to record it. So Columbia sent Bruce over to the Regency Hotel to interview Burton for some promotion. A union recording engineer had to be there and Bruce asked me to tag along too to make sure the recording aspect was up to snuff.

So... 11 AM and we passed through the gilded lobby of The Regency Hotel and up the mirrored elevator to the Penthouse.

Burton opened the door and, as we'd expected, at 11 AM, asked if we'd like to join him in a whiskey or two ... or three.

He was a terrific raconteur, a charming man but I couldn't help but wonder where The Most Beautiful Woman In The World was. I heard rustling behind one of the doors, but that was the only clue.

Then, as the interview drew to a close, the door opened and Liz Taylor glided out, with less than a full make-up job, wearing a flimsy peignoir and holding a very small dog.

(My son, Max, says that any dog small enough to punt can't rightfully be called a dog.)

It was then that I noticed something I hadn't noticed when I came in: on the floor all around the periphery of this penthouse apartment, festooned with priceless furniture of the periods of Louis the 14th, 15th, 16th and all subsequent Louis's, was DOG SHIT.

And of course it was obvious that, if you're Elizabeth Taylor, you can't just go out on the sidewalk to walk your dog.

> The Great Leveler: if you're a dog owner in New York City, the rich and the poor, the anonymous and the famous, ALL have to deal with dog shit.

She said hello in her buttery, little-girl voice and, too soon, we were out of there.

Bruce just wrote a very readable autobiography but I'll just tell you one story he told me that isn't in his book.

> He was a great lover of comedy and he attributed that to his formative years.
> He grew up as a kid next to the Palisades Amusement Park in New Jersey. His house was separated from the roller coaster by only a chain-link fence. Every night as he fell asleep he would hear the sound of the roller coaster climbing up: Clack clack clack clack clack clack ...
> Then, a moment after it crested, the screams:
> "Aaaaaahhhhhhh!!!!!!!!!!"
>
> Every five minutes.
> Slapstick.

Bruce was a wonderfully warm, supportive and encouraging guy. He was a big jazz fan, as became apparent later in his leadership at Columbia, Blue Note and Capitol records. He signed Herbie Hancock, Norah Jones, Wynton Marsalis and Stan Getz as well as popsters Willie Nelson, James Taylor and Anita Baker and many other talented artists.

During the last years of his life, he was beset with Parkinson's Disease But still, rolling around in his wheelchair and having difficulty speaking clearly, he continued to help artists and even organized a top-flight jazz festival in the assisted living residence where he spent his last days.

Bruce died while I was writing this. He was the best.

***

The top 2 floors at 799 Seventh Avenue housed the recording studios and editing rooms. This was the domain of the engineers. Some were recording engineers, some were assistant recording engineers, some were mixing engineers, and some were mastering engineers.

The recording engineers were, I suppose, the royalty and they each had their specialties.
Frank Laico, pictured earlier with producer Mike Berniker, was the premier pop music producer, responsible for Tony Bennett, Andy Williams, Barbra Streisand, Ray Coniff and all that.

Ascot-wearing, pipe-smoking, Austria-born Fred Plaut recorded classical music as well as Lieberson's Broadway show albums. He didn't really like working on pop albums.
I remember one time when Fred was the engineer assigned to work with me on a pop album. I asked him to turn up the drums. Fred didn't like drums. So he said, "Ja." and turned his hand which seemed to grasp the round rotary knob that controlled the drums. But actually he faked it: his hand moved while the knob underneath didn't.

But the Young Turks, the upstarts, the prodigies were Roy Hallee and Fred Catero.

Columbia was very slow to get into rock 'n roll and the music of young people but, when they did, it was Roy and Fred who led the charge. They were delighted to experiment with new sounds, new ways of recording.

They'll each figure in this story later.

Each of the mixing engineers had his own mix room on the 6th floor. You had to book appointments with them and some were so in demand that you had to book a month ahead of time. All of them taught me so much in those hours I spent in their mix rooms.

It was at this point that I came to a fork in the road. Coming from a musical background with only a passing knowledge of electronics, I had to ask others about equalization, limiting and compression, different microphones, etc. But I soon realized that engineering didn't excite me. I had the choice then to get deeper into the technical side—new developments in microphones and other gear—or to spend whatever learning time I had on music and how to lead a recording project smoothly and efficiently to its conclusion.

I decided on the latter course of action, leaving the technical stuff to whatever engineer/partner would accompany me on any particular safari through the jungles of making an album.

TRACK 11 – THE TRIAL

By now I had picked up some of the universal written code used by producers and engineers in the studio to abbreviate the relative success of takes.

You'd write on the recording log sheet: fs (false start), bd (short breakdown), BD (longer breakdown), INC (incomplete take), CT (complete take).

Producers were allowed to do that. And to direct the recording sessions. But, other than that, hands off!

> Since Columbia was a union shop, it was forbidden for me to touch any equipment. I almost salivated with the urge to get my hands on those knobs and that tape. It would be a few years before I'd be able to do that.

This was the only piece of recording studio equipment that I was allowed to touch:

The International Brotherhood of Electrical Workers (the engineer's union) made it a venal sin for anyone other than a union engineer to touch the mixing board, a microphone or even a microphone stand.

If you were to touch one of those select objects, The Special Goddess of Engineers (I suppose that would be Elektra) would send a mega-volt bolt of lightning through the roof of Studio A and strike you dead while the union engineers shrugged their shoulders and said to themselves, "We warned him."

But I belonged to a union too. When I was in high school, in order to play at that strip joint, I had to join Local 52 of the American Federation of Musicians. So I figured I had a legitimate union-approved position in the recording studio.

I was about to experience first-hand the power of my musical brotherhood.

It started at one of the very first recording sessions I produced on my own: the soundtrack for a TV series called "The Reporter". The composer was Kenyon Hopkins, a jazz guy who'd written the score for "The Hustler" and "Twelve Angry Men". And among the players were some of my idols. Osie Johnson and Milt Hinton holding down the rhythm section, legendary horn players Zoot Sims, Ernie Royal, Clark Terry, Phil Woods, Urbie Green ...

I was in heaven.

But a problem arose on our second day of recording. The night before the session, NYC experienced one of those pre-dawn snowstorms that left the city under a blanket of white over a foot deep.
So, understandably, the three-hour session started more than an hour late.

It was the practice of Local 802, the musicians union, to occasionally send a representative to drop in on sessions unannounced to make sure there were no violations of union regulations.

That very afternoon a union rep, whom I shall call Bobby Greenfield cuz that was his name, showed up just as the end of our 2 PM-5 PM session approached.
We had one more tune to complete that day. So, with two minutes left, we hit it and we finished one minute after 5 o'clock.

As everyone packed up, Bobby said, "Do you want the guys for the rest of the overtime?"

Overtime?! Oh no, that would put us way over budget.

I said, "Jeez, we only went one minute over and we started late because of the snow and ..."

"You only booked the guys till 5 o'clock. You went over the three hours."

"But, but, but ...", I replied.

"You've got to pay the guys."

"Aw, come on, Bobby, cut the bullshit. Give the kid a break", said Barry Galbraith, wonderful guitar player and champion of 21-year-old fledgling producers.

Everyone left, the session was over but on my desk the next morning was a summons to appear before the union Trial Board in a week.

Cut to one week later.

There we were in front of the Local 802 Trial Board: Bobby Greenfield, Barry Galbraith and me. I had never been in any kind of court before and I remember thinking that this didn't seem like a "trial by one's peers" or anything I'd ever seen in a movie or on TV.

It was hard to imagine that my "peers" were in fact Brother Musicians. I couldn't imagine any of those tired old geezers blowing a horn, banging a drum or picking a guitar.

> The only picking going on was one of my judges more absorbed in picking his nose than hearing any testimony. And I might have imagined that another of them was lost in the memory of a beautiful adagio, eyes closed– – except he was snoring.

The trial was swift justice. In fact, to make things as swift as possible, the verdict had been decided <u>before</u> the trial.
After the trail, I walked back to the office and there on my desk, <u>mailed the day before the trial</u>, was the verdict.

Guilty. $50 fine.

I wish we musicians had a Goddess as protective as Elektra.

TRACK 12 – CHICAGO

After I'd put in some time in my apprenticeship in the pop music department, and had produced a few isolated sessions, somebody figured I was ready to be assigned an artist from Columbia's stellar roster for me to produce all of their albums on my own.

And that artist for my maiden voyage was Frankie Yankovic, "America's Polka King", and the scene of the crime was to be Chicago.

I flew out from New York, checked into a hotel and, early the next morning, went to the address of Columbia Records' studios in Chicago—surprisingly a slick, modern skyscraper.

Frankie was Slovenian. Beloved by all his fans. And this was his 50th birthday.

As the elevator rose, a distinctive smell intensified and, when the elevator doors opened to the eighth floor, the source was visible: kielbasa!

Some 50-year-old "groupies" had set up an impromptu kitchen in the eighth floor lobby to fix Frankie a Slovenian birthday feast.

When I went into the control room of the studio itself and met Jim Felix, the engineer, I was struck by the antiquated nature of the recording equipment. While Columbia in New York benefited from the up-to-date innovations of the research and development engineers there, the equipment in Chicago looked like it came out of the trenches of World War I.

Instead of a horizontal "desk", the controls were knobs on the face of a big metal box and if somebody reminded me that they were camouflage, I wouldn't argue the case. You expected the operator to say, "Captain, I'm not getting a signal from the platoon! I think the enemy must have cut the line!"

Frankie was famous for a big sound. And when I saw the studio set up, I understood how that came about:

He stood in the middle and pretty much just pumped out chords on his squeezebox with gusto. On one side of him, another musician played a Swiss musette accordion with a wonderfully sweet sound and, on the other side, was Joey Misculin, a teenage prodigy whose fingers danced over his accordion keys like ants on a hot plate.

So, in the stereo, it sounded like one huge accordion, Frankie's, and, unless you listened very carefully, he sounded like the most sensational accordion virtuoso imaginable.

The other musicians in the ensemble were Frank's piano player who had been with him forever, a father and son team playing bass and guitar, and, looking very out of place, a young drummer in his black suit, totally wasted, (and I mean totally wasted) who seemed to have just come from an all-night jazz jam and who was only there because he happened to be Slovenian.

Frankie was a nice man and he had managed to carve quite a considerable niche for himself among polka lovers. One of the ways he did this was to appear "Live, In Person" in several towns at once though they might be 100 miles apart.

He would book a band into each of those towns and, with a Cessna and a pilot, appear for one set in each town.

I did two albums with Frankie: "Movietime Polkas And Waltzes" and "Polkas And Waltzes Just For Fun". He was game for any novelty that would sell records, although he did have a tricky time with the lyrics to "Supercalifragilisticexpialidocious".

TRACK 13 – PAUL SIMON'S LEAST FAVORITE SONG

There was a great espirit de corps at 799 7th Ave. Even though we were a part of CBS, it was almost as if the parent corporation didn't know we existed. We were a wild, wacky wing, bustling around like bees, independent and creative.

So there was general displeasure when CBS collected our happy band and threaded us into several floors in the new corporate headquarters at 51 W. 52nd St. designed by famed and unpronounceable architect, Eero Saarinen.

Black Rock.

My new office, 10' x 10' was about the size of a large closet and, without any windows, just about as cheery.

A few months after our move to Black Rock, when CBS Corporate gave me the title of mere "Associate Producer", a guy in a suit in his early 30s came in to play a demo for me. His name was Nat Weiss.

> There was always a steady stream of people bringing demos of songs or singers to producers. Demos back then were on ten-inch acetates, which looked like records but were made of a softer material that wouldn't last as long. So a song-plugger (a publisher or manager) would have quite a few acetates pressed for his campaign to get the song recorded professionally.

Nat had played this demo for a lot of the other producers on our floor who had shown no interest in it but when the guy said he was "Brian Epstein's American Associate", I paid closer attention. After all, Brian Epstein was the Manager of Hottest Pop Music Act in the World—The Beatles.

> (Col. Tom Parker, Elvis's manager was, for the moment, not the Manager of Hottest Pop Music Act in the World because Elvis was temporarily in the Army.)

The demo wasn't bad but I hadn't yet had the nerve or the confidence to actually try to make a record out of any of the demos that came through my door. But this time? There was a lot about the song that I liked so ... Well, it was worth a shot.

By now, Bill Gallagher, an imposing ex – shoe-salesman known in the building as "The Pope", was in charge of the A&R department.

I screwed up my courage and went in and asked him for $2000 to record a demo.

"2000?", he chuckled. "Hell, Kid. Take 5."

So I did.

I went back to Columbia's former building, 799 Seventh Avenue, to record in the smaller of the two studios there, Studio D.

The song on the demo Nat brought me was "Red Rubber Ball" co-written by Bruce Woodley, from a band called The Seekers, and by Paul Simon (prior to Simon and Garfunkel) who, at the time, was poor and busking alone on the sidewalks of London.

> There were just three in the group: Tom Dawes, Don Danneman and Marty Fried, on bass, guitar and drums, respectively.
>
> But I had an arrangement in my head that needed another instrument to play a little riff between the verses.
> There was a B3 organ in the studio so I figured I'd play that riff on that.
>
> I imagined a tambourine part too.

(Note the earnest mien – a put-on for the photo.)

In addition I wanted to lift the last verse with a change of keys. "A modulation!", exclaimed rock critic Morgan Ames later, "a rarity in rock 'n roll."

I knew nothing then about mixing. But Freddie Catero, at that point still a mixing engineer, made the record sound great, particularly that tambourine.

Everything worked out right with that record: the choice of that song, the group's harmonies, the organ part, Freddie's mixing. Maybe it was just Beginner's Luck but the record came out great.

I still remember where I was when I first heard it coming out of the car radio and how wonderful that felt.

> Any pride in personal accomplishment that I had previously felt was dwarfed by the fact that I had succeeded on the playing field of grown-ups. And despite any successes I've had in my work since then, nothing has ever matched the spike of that thrill.

The Pope and his cardinals and bishops were excited about the potential sales of Red Rubber Ball. The band at the time was called The Frat Men or something equally collegiate but no one was particularly happy with that name.
Then here came some news: Brian Epstein himself was coming to America to give the band a New Name!

> Oh, boy. This was the guy who named The Beatles and managed them into worldwide super-success. Surely any name he would come up with would have considerable staying power.

So there we were, in Studio A, the big studio this time, recording some more songs to fill out an album that everyone was sure would be in demand– – and Brian showed up.

This was the night of the naming. A Rock Christening.

While we were recording, the illustrious Brian Epstein, the Beatles' manager, sat in the back of the control room listening, thinking, scribbling names on scraps of paper then balling them up and throwing them away as not good enough.

> "Boy, look at how hard he's working. This is going to be a great name." We could hardly concentrate on the recording.

Then, beaming, he produced the name: "The Cyrkle"—spelled funny like The Beatles.

Here's a photo of the guys expecting their new name.

And here they are <u>afterwards</u>.

Disappointed ...

Whenever "Red Rubber Ball comes up in conversation, people say, "Oh, I remember that record. But I can't remember the name of the group."

… Nice try, Brian.

> Paul Simon was asked if there was a song he'd regretted writing. He replied, "Red Rubber Ball". But I'm glad he wrote it.

The single was a huge hit. The record was the "cleanest" single of the year, meaning it had the least number of returns from record shops that had ordered it. It was flying off the shelves.

"Red Rubber Ball" flew up the charts too: Number Two with a bullet. A bullet meant exceptional popularity and, being Number Two, there was nowhere to go but the top of the list. We couldn't wait to see it at the very top of the charts next week.

So when the next Billboard came out we just about ripped it open to the page with the charts and there at Number One was … "My Baby Does The Hanky-Panky" by Tommy James and the Shondells!

> Now never mind what's a Shondell. How could this happen? I puzzled over this for years.

And then, a few years ago, Tommy James published his autobiography.

Now I don't know who bought his book. I <u>almost</u> did. But instead I went to Barnes & Noble, found the book in the racks, searched through the index for "Hanky-Panky" and there was the answer to my burning question.

Not only did Tommy James's <u>Baby</u> do the hanky-panky, Tommy James's <u>record company</u> did the hanky-panky.

"My Baby Does The Hanky Panky" at Number One.

It seems Roulette records was friendly with the mob—and, while we had been number two with a bullet, ironically bullets may have had something to do with it.

(What follows is hearsay. I didn't witness it myself but tales like this were so common in the record business that I believe it to be true:)

> Bruce Lundvall, my pal from Columbia Records, later on became the president of several major record companies. At one point he was sent to a small successful record label to woo them into the fold of his larger company. All the parties involved sat at a conference table to discuss the acquisition. When Bruce looked at their prospectus he noticed that there was nothing there with regard to promotion. He asked the owners of the small label, "What about your promotion department? I don't see it in these pages." One of the owners pulled a forty-five out of his jacket, laid it on the table and said, "<u>This</u> is our promotion department."

TRACK 14 – THE MEDIUM IS THE MASSAGE

1966 was the first of some really productive years for me. With the success of "Red Rubber Ball", I was released from my 10 by 10 cubicle and given a larger office with a window and a potted plant. And with that success, it was thought that I had some magic secret for success in pop music—which of course I didn't.

In the recording studio I was learning by experimentation. I was assigned various artists. I produced single records with artists who would later be successful, like Broadway star Bernadette Peters, jazz thrush Carol Sloane, and Bonnie Herman, a singer with a beautiful sound and absolutely perfect intonation who later used those gifts as the lead voice of Singers Unlimited.

> And lots of bands with names lost to history like "The Clefs Of Lavender Hill" (formerly two bands, "The Clefs" and "The Lavender Hill Mob"), "Thor's Hammer", "Duke's New Sound Band" and "The Fabulous Fakes".

Then there was Marshall McLuhan—of all people. In the 60s if you were at all aware, you knew who McLuhan was. He was the prophet of modern advertising and a very learned man with several professorships and books under his belt. Now he had authored, with graphic artist Quentin Fiore, a very popular paperback called, "The Medium Is the Massage". (That's not a typo.)

Jerry Agel, publisher of a magazine called "Books", was instrumental in putting McLuhan's book together and came into my office with the proposition of making a recording of it.

The idea sounded crazy enough and challenging enough to me and, when I brought the idea to Clive Davis, by then the company president, McLuhan's name was prestigious and appealed to him and so we got the green light.

> After all the elements had been recorded, Jerry Agel joined engineer Don Puluse and me in the mixing room and we assembled an album that followed the sequence of the book.

The next morning Jerry called me and said that it didn't make any sense for this to be such a linear record since part of what McLuhan was saying was that media was evolving from linearity into a more random deluge of information.

So we re-edited the album, cutting and pasting for humor and dramatic effect.

"The Medium Is The Massage" album found a small audience. But it was to figure in my life significantly a few more times .

TRACK 15 – THE MOST IMPORTANT DATE IN THE HISTORY OF ROCK 'N ROLL

I saw all this happen right before my eyes and it changed rock and roll forever.

There are several candidates for the honor of The Most Important Date In The History Of Rock 'n Roll: the day Sam Phillips recorded Elvis, when Dylan went electric, when Mick Jagger reached puberty…

But I think it was DECEMBER 25, 1966.

To explain, let's go back a couple of years before that to the appearance of The Beatles.

The popularity of The Beatles was HUGE! If you weren't around then, it would be hard for you to imagine. I'm too young to have witnessed the Bobby-Soxers craze over Frank Sinatra and I was a teenager when Elvis snared the hearts and fantasies of my female classmates.

The paths of both Elvis and Sinatra, despite their popularity, were controlled by Music Business executives, grown-ups who made their career decisions for them. The Beatles appeared during the emancipating years of The Sixties when, not only Women's Lib and Black Power were on the rise, but Kids' Lib was evident everywhere. Teenagers had new power. "Don't Trust Anyone Over Thirty".

Grown-ups (including record company execs) didn't understand the Beatles' immense popularity, and thus their power. Of course pubescent girls found them irresistibly cute. But The Beatles had ascended to a position of power in a grown-up world and, apart from the music they made, this caught the attention of young boys too.

> Prior to the immense popularity of those British Mop-Tops it wasn't a goal of the average teen lad to be a musician. Hard to believe today, isn't it? The life of a traveling pop musician could wear you out (and still can, in fact). Though a young man might have a girlfriend who saw through his temporary skin problems to the lovable swain underneath, it was nothing like the wild crowd of teenage girls who were Beatles fans, just aching to satisfy the plea, "I Want To Hold Your Hand".

Once young boys saw how popular and powerful they could be once they strapped on a guitar or sat behind a set of skins, the floodgates opened.

> Now, as it happened, in the 1950's an electronics inventor named Leo Fender had perfected a solid-body electric guitar and eventually established The Fender Guitar Company, a small outfit dedicated to manufacturing those instruments exclusively.

With The Beatles, the sudden surge of adolescent interest in electric guitars caught the attention of CBS execs who, in around 1966, bought Fender. And the following Christmas morning, under 47% of the Christmas Trees in America (and don't bother checking that number because I made it up), instead of the Rollfast bicycle or the Rawling's baseball mitt, there was a brand-new Fender Guitar!

December 26, 1966

As I see it, The Most Important Date In The History Of Rock 'n Roll

After awhile Junior started looking for friends to start a band.

The Beatles   NOT The Beatles

They grew their hair long. They wore funny clothes. At high school dances they played the few songs they knew to a chorus of female screams of moist adulation. And they all had brand-spanking-new Fender electric guitars.

Those teens were also major record-buyers. And, in the U.S., Capitol Records was the lucky record company reaping the revenue from The Four Lads From Liverpool. All the other labels were green with greed and envy and wanted to cash in too.

So imagine, if you will, a golf course:

> The president of a record company is playing golf with his buddy, a manager of musical acts. And by the time they reach the 18th green, the record company president can no longer contain himself.

> Record Co. President: "Jeez! I can no longer contain myself. Capitol is reaping the revenue from those 4 Lads From Liverpool. I wish we had an act like that on our label."

> Manager: "Well, you're in luck. I've got just the act for you: 4 Lads From Piscataway. They look just like the Beatles: same clothes, same hair, same screaming girls."

Well, all that was TRUE.
But it didn't go much further than that.

> Although a few of those kids later proved that they had enough talent (and luck) to succeed, 99.99% of them didn't. (Of course by now you're familiar enough with this author to know that that number is an approximation.)

But the economy was booming and the record companies were desperate to get some of what Capitol had.
So million-dollar contracts were thrown at these new bands in the hope that some of them would have that mysterious je ne sais quoi that would sell records like The Beatles.

So now potentially EVERY KID was a rock musician. And recording studios across the country were FLOODED with these new groups. My bosses at Columbia Records would drop some untested act at my feet and say, "Here's a sow's ear. Gimme a silk purse."

And it became the privilege of producers like me to try to extract something approximating music from them.

Let's refer back to The Beatles for a moment.

> Those 4 Liverpudlians were <u>not</u> like the 4 Lads from Piscataway, Ronkonkoma or Cucamonga. The Beatles had been together as a band for many years before they ever saw the inside of a recording studio.

> And when they eventually <u>did</u> go into a studio, they played their songs in front of microphones, every one playing at the same time, exactly as they had in the clubs.
> They could do that. They were pros.

But these brand-new bands from Massapequa, Ypsilanti and Appalachicola were <u>not</u> pros. They'd show up in the recording studio and, like The Beatles, they were expected to all play at the same time. But they couldn't. They were new at this; they could hardly play a song through once without mistakes.

> Maybe the drummer and maybe the bass player would play their parts right while the lead guitar player might be hours away from a passable guitar solo.
> So everyone would have to do take after take after take while the guitar player was trying to play a passable solo and, believe me, it was tedious!

So there we were: first The Beatles, then a proliferation of Beatle Wannabes, money in the economy, and a plague of bands-that-shouldn't-be-bands.

A real problem that needed resolution.

And then it got interesting because, yes,
Necessity Is the Mother Of Invention.

Whether or not it was a blessed coincidence, at the same time that this problem had become epidemic in the studios, some recording equipment designers were wrestling with another problem.

For years, some recording artists (most notably the guitarist, Les Paul) had been experimenting with layering instruments on top of each other. They had accomplished this by "ping-ponging" back and forth between 2 tape machines. The results were exciting and innovative but, because of having to record back and forth on new recording tape each time, a lot of tape "hiss" would build up until the results were very noisy.
Then some engineer came up with a brilliant idea. What if it could all happen on one machine, on one section of recording tape?

And 8 track tape was born.

(This is not the 8 track tape cartridge for your car that was the rage in the Seventies until cassettes came into the picture. This is 8 track recording tape which allowed players to easily overdub their parts one-at-a-time on 8 parallel tracks on a single section of tape.)

So, for instance, when I was assigned to make a record with a still-wet-behind-the-ears group, I was suddenly able to record the guys who were able to play their parts on a few of the 8 tracks and leave the other tracks for the guitar player to try his solo over and over again. While the rest of the guys went home.

(Or, more likely, they'd go into the control room, light up a doobie and giggle for the rest of the session.)

And then it got REAL interesting.

The appearance of 8 track and other more sophisticated developments in recording led, in turn, to a major change in the newly-recorded records THEMSELVES.

8-track recording tape was a blessing for us producers. Now we had extra tracks to allow room for the mistakes made by these new, lightly-talented artists with their new instruments.

But more creatively-gifted artists didn't need those additional tracks to compensate for their failings!

They didn't have any failings.

Instead they used those new tracks to enrich their records, to paint a much richer audio picture – with background voices, percussion, horns, strings, anything they wanted.

And this new, multi-track recording then led to a totally new ART-FORM.

We can call it a "More Produced Record".

> For instance, the records The Beatles made at first, like "Meet the Beatles", were repetitions of their live performances and analogous to documentary films.
> But then, with multi-track recording came "Rubber Soul" and "Sergeant Pepper."

> More Produced Records.

JOHN SIMON

And it all started with The Most Important Date In The History Of Rock And Roll.

***

One of my first experiences working on a More Produced Record was Simon and Garfunkel's "Bookends" album.

TRACK 16 – PAUL AND ARTIE

The Pope called me into his office.

"Kid, we've got an important project for you. CBS just bought the Fender Guitar company so we need you to write and produce a Guitar Instruction Record."

"Well, sure, but there's a small problem: I don't play the guitar."

"Perfect. You, yourself represent the target audience."

He wouldn't take no for an answer and so I bungled through inventing a Guitar Instruction Method with the help of some guitar players I knew.

The odds of someone who doesn't play the guitar writing a worthwhile guitar instruction book are pretty slim, but apparently my bosses didn't think so. The result was a release that held the record for the "dirtiest" record of that year in that it got the <u>most</u> returns from the record shops that ordered it.

Even though that disaster should have challenged their faith in me and, maybe in desperation, they assigned me to produce Simon and Garfunkel.

I say "in desperation" because, since their huge successes with "Sounds of Silence", their album called "Parsley, Sage, Rosemary and Thyme" and their music for the movie, "The Graduate", they were able to coast on those successes for awhile.

But Columbia wanted to cash in on their popularity as quickly as possible and no producer had been able to get them to speed up their output in order to get a new album out of them.

I enjoyed working with them a lot. They were smart, hip, a little neurotic ... I was familiar with that combination.
We had a few things in common, starting with the simple fact that Paul's father and my father were both named Lou Simon and played string instruments.
And Artie and I had, at one time, each considered careers as architects.

Shortly after meeting them, they invited me to go along to the Forest Hills tennis stadium on Long Island where they were playing a concert.

Of all the acts I've worked with before and since, I never saw artists who were as comfortable and relaxed performing as they. It was all so casual. The transition from their ease before their show into their ease onstage was seamless. Their performance was just like a conversation with the audience. Maybe it was because they'd been performing together for so long—since they started out in school as the musical duo, Tom and Jerry.

Clive Davis passionately urged Paul and Artie to go into the studio and they finally agreed. Beforehand I met with them and they outlined their ideas for an overdub on "Save The Life Of My Child", a song they'd already recorded.

They wanted violins but softer and lower so I suggested muted violas. Then they had some brass punctuation in mind and some percussion as well. They sang a few lines for me and I wrote out an arrangement.

The Standard Operating Procedure for a recording session before the proliferation of inexperienced rock acts was to record 4 songs in 3 hours. And that was easy for most recordings because the professional musicians could read any music you put in front of them and they played without making mistakes.

I knew that Paul and Artie were pros but, since we were working together for the first time, I figured I'd allow a full three-hour session to overdub those three elements on that one song, the first hour for the strings, the second for the brass and the last hour for the percussion.

Plenty of time.

The night of the session arrived. Twelve viola players showed up and, thinking there must have been a mistake, they immediately checked with their booking services (because usually there were three times as many violins as violas at a session plus a couple of cellos). Then I conducted them through the chart I'd written for them.

After that initial run-through, as the viola players checked their intonation, a voice from the control room said,

"What was that?"

"What was what?", I said.

"That sound", said Artie and Paul.

"That was just the guys tuning up", I said.

"Well, forget the chart. We like that instead."

"What th—"

We tried to replicate that random tuning-up for hours and never got it the way they wanted.

And, on top of that, the brass players showed up in the lobby and the percussionists after them and consequently they had to wait a long time for their opportunities in front of the mics—which they were very happy about because their union scale overtime hours were making their mental cashboxes ring.

This extravagance was very new to me and I came to find out why—at least I think I know why.

The way most record contracts work is this: the record company will pay for the cost of recording: musicians and studio costs. But then they withhold paying the artist any royalty money until they make that investment back from record sales. So, in actuality, the artist is at first paying for the cost of recording. That's pretty much standard.

I think I heard that Paul and Artie's manager, Mort Lewis, when they made their initial deal with Columbia Records, got the record company to waive that arrangement on the basis that, since there were only the 2 of them with no additional musicians, recording costs would be insignificant. So Columbia would pay for all the recording costs and Paul and Artie wouldn't have to pay for a thing.

(That's technically Hearsay, but I've heard it from enough insiders to believe it myself. Besides it makes sense.)

So, after Tom Wilson's rock overdubs on "Sounds of Silence", when Simon and Garfunkel's sound had come to include any number of additional musicians, the duo never had to pay for a thing

And, since all of the costs of recording were now gratis, they were free to experiment at no expense to themselves.

And experiment they did.
We continued to work on that song, "Save the Life of My Child" at another session at the cavernous 30th St. studio and it was there that I saw my first synthesizer.

Bob Moog the inventor of the synthesizer, showed up with one of the first prototypes.

He pronounced his name to rhyme with "rogue", but he wasn't a rogue at all. He was an unpretentious guy with a little bit of the mad inventor about him because he was still developing his machine. He would fumble with a fist full of patch cords plugging them in various holes like a harried operator at an old telephone switchboard.

His rig was a lot smaller than the roomful of tubes that my old professor, Milton Babbitt had worked with earlier. But, compared to the synths of today which you can hold in your hand, what he brought to 30th Street was enormous—about the size of three mattresses.

The guys asked me to play that synthesizer to create the bass line and some other weird effects on "Save The Life Of My Child" and on "Fakin' It". I was real happy to be involved in playing something on their record.

I really can't leave out engineer Roy Hallee in any mention of Simon and Garfunkel.

When I got to Columbia Records in 1963 I was made aware that this was definitely a union shop. Seniority counted: it took a long time for union members to eventually get promoted from assistant engineers to recording engineers.
But then, I saw the exception: Roy Halee.

Boy-faced, cheerful Roy Halee was decades younger than the other recording engineers yet there he was at the recording console enthusiastically riding the faders and tweaking the knobs at the sessions of the artists who were aiming at a youngish audience.

I don't know how he got behind the console in the recording studio, leap-frogging over other union guys with seniority. It happened before I got there. My guess is that someone simply saw his talent and said, "Let's break the rules and move him up and the union be damned."

Roy loved to experiment. He got that huge snare drum backbeat sound for Simon & Garfunkel's records through some combination of tape delay and the empty stone stairwells of 799 Seventh Avenue.

Sound quality was important to the artists too. I was struck by how many times Paul would change to a fresh set of guitar strings in the course of our work on "Bookends". The result was always a beautiful clear tone.

And, for that album, Artie would spend countless hours out on the street with a Nagra tape machine, recording old people. On occasional other days, the three of us would meet in the studio to work on songs that formed the nucleus of the album.

But, back then when "Bookends" was coming together, despite my being "new blood" as their producer, Paul and Artie were still slowpokes in the studio.

So Bob Johnston took over "Bookends" while Columbia assigned another artist to me.

TRACK 17 – LEONARD COHEN

A couple of days ago as I was typing this, a Federal Express truck pulled up to my house in the woods and delivered a huge rectangular box. Inside was a lot of padding and another box and inside of that careful wrapping was a large envelope. By this time I decided to look at the return address. It was from the Grammy organization. In the envelope was a large certificate suitable-for-framing announcing that Leonard Cohen's first album had been certified as something worthy of certification according to Grammy with a letter congratulating me on the record's being certified.

Illustration showing the relative size of the Grammy certificate.
(Margin of error = 5000%)

Over the years, the Grammy organization has presented me with a few frames containing records coated with certain precious metals, gold being the most common. When I actually put my first one, for "Bookends" on the turntable, I discovered that the label bearing the title of the album I worked on had been pasted on an Andy Williams Christmas Album.

When I met Leonard, he told me how he had been signed by John Hammond but John kept postponing recording sessions and Leonard felt like he was festering in the Chelsea Hotel—so he begged Columbia to assign another producer to him.

He had already recorded at least one song, "The Stranger Song", that featured the difficult, insistent triplet pattern that he had mastered with the fingers of his right hand.

> The techniques that a musician becomes proficient in are called his "chops".
> Leonard referred to his triplet technique as his "chop" (singular).

He was different from the other artists I knew. They were kids. He was a grown-up. And an intellectual. He was already a published poet.

When we were to get together to talk about recording I suggested getting out of Manhattan, giving him a break from The Chelsea and going to my folks' house while they were off somewhere out of town.

We drove out to Norwalk and he played me some of his songs. After we talked a while, I was tired and went to sleep but when I awoke in the morning I discovered that Leonard, the curious aesthete, had stayed up all night browsing through the books in my father's library.

I was interviewed for a bio of Leonard. So, since they're my words, I figure I can reprint them here.

... "Suzanne" is fucking gorgeous. I love this track—the strings and the girls together with the vocal and guitar make a lush blanket of sound. This and "Hey, That's No Way To Say Goodbye" both have a guitar line in thirds with the vocal.

... "The Stranger Song" made me think about his lyrics. Although Bob Dylan paved the way for the lyricists who followed him, in that he got an audience to accept lyrics that were more thought-ful, less banal than the average pop lyric, Leonard's seem to show more finesse. His scansion is stricter, his rhymes truer as a rule. Whereas Dylan's language had a connection to 'the people', in the tradition of Woody Guthrie, blues and folk, Leonard's lyrics reveal a more educated, exposed, literate poetry.

...I also like the humor in the lyrics of "One of Us Cannot Be Wrong". They have the undercurrent of ardent young lust, but they're so funny at the same time. As for the questionable taste of the ending with the recorder, the whistle and Leonard screeching way up high, what can I say? We were young."

(from "I'm Your Man")

But the thing that pleased me the most about this album was that I would have the chance to do some real arrangements of my own, not like simply taking dictation from Paul and Artie. This would be my first chance to do that.

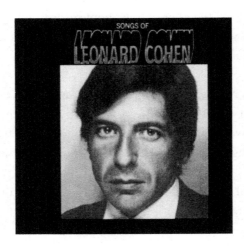

Because so many of Leonard's songs seemed to be either about women or addressed to them, I felt a real female presence in all the material.

So instead of using horns or strings for the musical lines that accompanied his vocals, I used wordless female voices, mostly sung by Nancy Priddy, my girlfriend at the time, who was uncredited – until now.

These were the years when I began to get very busy in the studio. So when Leonard told me he'd like to scrap some of the work we'd done and complete the album on his own, that was okay with me.

Sort of apologetically, he said to me, "There's no accounting for taste".

Subsequently, for "So Long, Marianne" and "Teachers" Leonard added some exotic instruments played by members of the band, "Kaleidoscope" featuring multi-instrumentalist, David Lindley.

In spite of our differences in taste as far as the arrangements, there was not a speck of animosity between Leonard and me.

My work with him was years before his immersion in Buddhism, not to mention his subsequent reputation as "the man in black" (sharing that handle with Johnny Cash). In our time together he was cheerful, funny, very rarely "dark". And, with his wit and intelligence , he was a joy to be around.

> As with some others in this book, Leonard passed on while I was putting these recollections together.
> Some say that the very rigorous touring schedule he organized for himself in his last years was out of financial need due to having been embezzled. Personally, I'm guessing that he also might have felt a need to just "get out there", stir people's thoughts and raise their consciousness.

> Or maybe he was tired.

TRACK 18 – BLOOD, SWEAT AND AL

Then I met Al Kooper...
Columbia had signed Al's band to the label and Clive Davis assigned me to produce them.

The Nairobi Trio again?

Blood, Sweat And Tears was a big horn band that leaned toward the powerful sound of bands like James Brown's, but with more intricate arrangements.

Al soon opened my eyes to something that changed my life. He said I should leave Columbia Records and become an independent, freelance producer.

I hardly knew they existed. I didn't even know that independent producers got royalties! This sounded a lot better than being a staff producer and, getting nothing beyond your salary, even if you made a hit
record.

> And besides I preferred being on my own and not being told, for
> instance, to write a guitar instruction book.

Al painted a pretty picture so I quit my job and produced Blood, Sweat
And Tears as an independent producer, working for an independent production company—in this case, run by Aaron Schroeder.

Back row: Dick Halligan (trombone), Fred Lipsius (alto sax) 2nd row:
Bobby Colomby (drums), Al, Steve Katz
(guitar), Jim Fielder (bass) Front row: Jerry Weiss and Randy
Brecker (trumpets) —with their mini-doppelgangers—

(Al and Steve had recently been members of The Blues Project. Bobby was the younger brother of Harry Colomby, Thelonious Monk's manager. Randy had come from Horace Silver's band.)

The sessions went well. They were fun.

I mentioned in the context of that marathon Paul & Artie session that the recording pros of the Fifties and early Sixties were easily capable of recording 4 songs in 3 hours without mistakes. This was also true with the guys in Blood, Sweat & Tears. They were all proficient professionals who could record without making mistakes.

And, meanwhile, 8-track recording machines had appeared in the studios. I'm not sure, but I suspect we recorded the BS&T album on 8-track.

One thing I do know for sure is that it was someone's idea (not mine—I don't know a decibel from Tinkerbell) to double the horns; that is to record the parts twice, one on top of the other. This gave the horn sound the consistent power that was part of BS&T's identity. This was a new recording concept at the time.

Al's choice of tunes (including his own) was impeccable. Almost all of the horn arrangements were the brain children of Fred Lipsius, the alto sax player in the band. You'd have to coax that fact out of Freddie who is Mr. Modesty.

The only horn line I <u>think</u> was not his is the catchy phrase at the end of "I Can't Quit Her". I say, "I <u>think</u>" because Randy Brecker thinks <u>he</u> came up with it and I think <u>I</u> did.

In the words of my final and greatest wife, C.C., "Memory is a Tricky Sidekick".

One night, after we'd gotten a terrific take of a song, the assistant engineer forgot to lock the reel of tape tightly to the recording machine and, when he rewound it, we watched it spiral up in the air and blast itself to smithereens. He was shaking with mortification, possibly fearing he might lose his cushy union job of just pushing "start" and "stop" on a tape machine. But we weren't bothered at all. We were amused.

The band was so good it was easy to get an even better take right away.

I remember a few other Al things, all post-BS&T:

1. While we were recording Al's solo album some years later, whenever the engineer and I would have to work for awhile by ourselves without Al, he would retreat to a hot tub elsewhere in the studio building, in the company of several nubile Hollywood misses who seemed to have come from the ubiquitous TV ads for Hollywood swimming pool paraphernalia. I burned with envy.

2. And in Al's L.A. house he had so many outfits that he had a dry cleaning conveyor belt installed in his closet.

3. Al has always had a good sense of how to attract attention for publicity. When he was temporarily on staff at Columbia, he wanted to give promotional copies of a record he'd made to DJs and Program Directors and attempted to persuade the Promotion Department to hire Andre, The Giant to do it (literally a huge celebrity).

Al tells me it didn't work out because Andre couldn't fit in a taxi.

TRACK 19 — "HELP! MY GUITAR'S ON FIRE!"

1967, the year that might be considered the advent of "The Sixties", was a Year of Change for me.

At Columbia, Goddard Lieberson, the fabled president of Columbia Records had recently been kicked upstairs within the CBS colossus and Clive Davis had taken his place.

Goddard's impeccable and erudite taste had marked the product stream that the label had turned out. But now, here was Rock and Roll, this new, raucous music that kids were buying and Columbia as yet had little part in it.

So, even though Rock Music may not have reflected Clive's personal taste, the profit motive prevailed and Clive pursued rock bands energetically.

Apparently, he also pursued some other, more personal interests energetically including using the record company's funds to partially fund his son's bar mitzvah and some greater improprieties for which a couple of Columbia employees a few levels down from Clive actually went to jail. Clive didn't go to jail.

(All that happened after I had left the company so my information is, admittedly, hearsay. Colorful as it is, it would be inadmissible in court. But I had to laugh when I saw a poster in a record exec's office that said boldly "Free Clive".)

But then the record business was never held up as the quintessence of transparency.

1967 was a Year of Leaving for me.
I left my job, I left my first marriage, I left New York.

I was on my way out of Columbia when the Monterey Pop Festival was announced. Though it has been eclipsed in rock history by the bigger and crazier Woodstock Festival two years later, Monterey was the first big rock festival.

Paul and Artie were going.
Columbia would buy me a plane ticket.
Sounded like fun.
So I went.

I had done a little work in LA before. It was the West Coast entertainment center. Columbia had a satellite staff there headed up by Irv Townsend who seemed to me to be a satellite Goddard Lieberson.

But a new West Coast music scene was birthing in and around San Francisco which gave new depth to the phrase, "laid-back." While LA was established and corporate, San Francisco was organic, home-grown, of the people. It seemed to be the unforced, logical outgrowth of the hippie culture.

Of all that I heard and saw over that Monterey weekend, I was most surprised by seeing classy Goddard Lieberson share a joint proffered by Paul and Artie in their hotel room. I was so naïve.

The Festival performances were great but far more interesting to me was the activity in the performers' backstage tent. A lot of the performers, stars in their respective genres and locales, were meeting each other for the first time.

It reminded me of an airport hub where flights from all over the world were experiencing a brief weather delay and consequently micro-cultures were mixing.

> An interesting contrast: in that tent was Tiny Tim playing precious little 50 year old ditties on his miniature ukulele while, 100 feet away on the stage, electric guitars were screaming in agony.

Although more than 30 acts performed during the 3 day festival, I remember only a few clearly.

Otis Redding. I'd never heard of him before. He delivered his lyrics with a sincerity that completely won me over and, at the same time, he had an energy that was so strong, but just-below-the-surface, generally resisting the temptation to overplay it.

I'd also never heard Ravi Shankar before. In his matinee performance, he played a mesmerizing raga. I closed my eyes and listened to music that suited Monterey's afternoon sunshine as comfortably as I imagined it would have in India.

The appearances by The Who and Jimi Hendrix weren't mesmerizing in the same way. They were major league artists who played their hits.

But then they set about destroying their instruments!

I don't remember which act went first but I certainly recall Hendrix biting his guitar strings instead of picking them, then setting his guitar on fire with lighter fluid. And Pete Townshend of The Who smashing his guitar to bits while Keith Moon tried to turn his drum set back into the raw materials from which it was made.

I was shocked! I'd never seen nor contemplated anything like that. I thought, "What Is Music Coming To?"

Why did they do that? What were they destroying? Was it a demonstration of protest against the Fender Guitar Company and, by extension, Big Business as a whole?

Or was it an inevitable consequence when youthful icons have the opportunity to demonstrate the fierce independence of their generation? After all, this was the era of liberation: Women's Lib, Black Liberation, sexual liberation, Down with The Establishment…

> *"T-t-t-talking 'bout My Generation".*
>
> (Pete Townshend, 1965)

I saw and heard a lot of rock lyrics in those years and it seemed that a common lyric was some variation on that message of "My Generation": "Mommy and Daddy suck."

And I didn't recall that sentiment having been as common in popular song before the advent of rock and roll.

There had been the "classy" songs of the 1940's and earlier. Songs with sophisticated, carefully crafted lyrics sung by Sinatra and Ella Fitzgerald. Then, in the Fifties, I remember a spate of really featherweight lyrics: "How Much Is That Doggie In The Window", "Come-on A-My House", "Volare".

But this new teen anger in music? That was new.

JOHN SIMON

Seeing Jimi and The Who go ballistic with their instruments seemed to me to indicate a sea change in the national mood.

And young people, eager to communicate with one another, now had a vehicle to express that anger and frustration.

Rock music was the medium for that message.

TRACK 20 – THE FIRST CLASS LOUNGE

The Monterey Festival crowd grew smaller below me.
In a few minutes I would take over the controls of the little Piper Cub and watch the rolling hills of the Monterey peninsula slip by below, I felt like Snoopy chasing The Red Baron in the Peanuts cartoon. But not for long. The actual pilot let me fly the plane only for a few minutes just for the thrill.

I was taking a break from the festival and we were puddle–jumping to SFO where I was to meet Peter Yarrow (of Peter, Paul and Mary) for an interview in United's first class lounge. P, P&M were on their way to Japan.

I had been recommended to Peter as someone who could help with the music for a movie he was making with cameraman Barry Feinstein, formerly Mary's husband.

> The recommender was actually my colleague at Columbia Records, another producer named Ed Kleban who was a fascinating fellow. Ed had gone to high school with Peter.
> Ed was a nice guy. Sweet man. His uncle was a V.P. at Columbia which is how he ended up there.

Ed's first assignment was not in New York City but in LA and his first job there was to pick up Igor Stravinsky at his home and drive him to the Columbia offices.

Now this wouldn't seem like a difficult assignment except for the fact that Ed was raised in New York City and barely knew how to drive. And when I say "barely", I mean "barely". And California freeways are not exactly Driver Training courses.
Ed thought, "Oh, great. I'm going to go down in history as the man who killed Igor Stravinsky."

Some years after I left Columbia Records, I heard that Ed had something you might call a nervous breakdown. He told me he was afraid to leave the block where he lived. He had to quit his job but the one activity he stuck with was the BMI Musical Theater Workshop, a writing program for aspiring Broadway composers and lyricists. The happy ending is that, through that workshop, nutty as he had become, he wrote the lyrics for "A Chorus Line" and became a zillionaire from it.

Kleban   Yarrow

Back to Peter Yarrow.
United's First-Class Lounge (I'd never been in one before.) was like an exclusive clubroom with over-stuffed leather chairs and magazines about

business and newspapers about business and cocktail napkins about business.

Drinks were free because this was a place for First Class People.

Into this sacred setting stormed Peter, bursting with warm energy and good humor. I loved that he busted through that stuck-up environment with something that seemed to me more alive. He was great.

> With his considerable clout with Warner Brothers Records, he had arranged for a record playback system to be delivered to the lounge. A WB underling set it up and disappeared into the general terminal to join the Lower Class People out there.

For my audition for Peter, I brought along "The Medium Is The Massage" album I did based on the Marshall McLuhan book. I figured it was the only thing close to cinematic in my box of oeuvres at that point.

Peter had a streak of the zany too. He appreciated the album and we set up a time to start work on the movie in a place called Woodstock.

TRACK 21 — A FISH STORY

Meanwhile, one of the bands that made big news at the Monterey Pop Festival was Big Brother And The Holding Company featuring a dynamic singer named Janis Joplin. Janis's potential appealed to Albert Grossman and he took over their management.

Albert was like no other manager at the time. Most managers wore suits because they had to deal with "suits". As he appeared earlier in the preface, Albert's copious belly was sometimes bracketed by suspenders. His head had those Ben Franklin glasses in front and a gray ponytail in the back. He looked older than he was. He had a good sense of humor. He was smart. He was a dealmaker. He was fiercely protective of his artists in the face of entertainment monoliths. He made mega-deals for them, co-incidentally making mega-bucks for himself.

Nobody got the best of him. He was a force.

He was Bob Dylan's and Peter, Paul and Mary's manager and it was through Peter that we met. Albert had owned a famous folk club in Chicago called The Gate Of Horn. He had managed artists in an arrangement with his longtime partner from Chicago, John Court, but that partnership was dissolving. While Albert had been responsible for the business end of their partnership, the musical side of their company, Grosscourt Productions, was John's bailiwick.

> I remember my first significant conversation with Albert. It was shortly after Monterey. We were walking down the sidewalk in New York City. After Peter Yarrow gave me his stamp of approval, Albert asked if I would work with some of his artists. He said, and I'll never forget this quote: "You scratch my back and I'll scratch yours."

That was a vague aphorism, hard to pin down, and it would foretell the vague business arrangements I would have with Albert in future years.

> But, all in all, I have to thank Albert for a few really significant things, like getting me a record deal to record my own songs and leading me to work with some wonderful artists.

Big Brother And The Holding Company had been signed to Bobby Shad's Mainstream Records but, after the Monterey Pop Festival, Albert convinced Clive Davis at Columbia to buy out that Mainstream contract. Memory tells me that rumors had the buy-out figure pegged at a million bucks.

Since I was Albert's new Music Guy, a few weeks after the Monterey Festival he and I flew out to San Francisco to meet with and listen to the band.

> We all met in one of Albert's favorite restaurants (Albert was a connoisseur of restaurants.). Gordon Lightfoot was there too so he corroborated the story I'm about to tell.

This was a very upscale Chinese restaurant and everyone was a little confused about what to order so Albert just took over and what the waiters brought out was a HUGE fish—whole from head to tail.
Immediately the guys in Big Brother started earnestly fighting over who would get to eat the fish's <u>eyes</u>!

So I said to Toto, "We're not in Kansas anymore."

I was from the NYC culture and its self-importance had convinced me that Manhattan was the center of the universe. So I hadn't bothered acquainting myself with what was going on in this San Francisco hodge-podge or in the towns around it.

But now, in San Francisco to check out Janis and her band more carefully, I got a better look around.

Life had taken me to LA a couple of times. But San Francisco appeared a lot different from LA.

LA looked picture-postcard-perfect: palm trees, beaches, warm weather, celebrities, convertibles, blonds. Except for the fact that the smog outdoors made your eyes bleed, it was utopian.

But there was a difference: LA's entertainment industry was run by grown-ups. In San Francisco, the kids had taken over the school. It was more improvised and home-spun than LA. Not as smooth. Gritty.

And that grit was apparent on the first day of rehearsal with this new band.

TRACK 22 – JANIS

I went with Albert to the address we were given. It was an old warehouse.

We know a lot of pop stars by their uncommon first names alone: Elvis, Aretha, Madonna, Cher ... And then there are the more common names: Ray, Ella, Jimi, Bruce ... Each of them has solid-ified a hold on a fairly first name.

It would take quite a star to usurp the first-name identity of the person we know simply as "Janis."

A lot of her fans would have given a vital piece of their physical corpus to be in her presence. That opportunity fell to me.
And I got to retain all of my body parts.

People ask me the inevitable question:
"What was Janis Joplin really like?"

Lord, who knows! Books, movies, songs, fan clubs, T-shirts, posters, plays, photos, articles, imitators ... It seems that, in the rock and roll morgue, her post mortem is longer than most.
The first time I saw her was at the Monterey Pop Festival, both onstage and backstage, but, aside from her volcanic personality, she had made no particular musical impression on me.

Now at that first rehearsal, I had a better look.

She was not of course alone.

James, Peter, Janis, Sam, Dave
(note the photo credit: the future Mrs. Paul McCartney)

Peter Albin was the bass player in the band who often stepped up to be the band's business representative – which was fine because, in the 60s, hippie business representatives were held to pretty low standards: he was as stoned as the rest.

But James Gurley gave the best impression of a stoner. Because he was. I was led to believe, whether they were pulling my leg or not, that when James wanted to learn how to play the guitar he bought one and just went out into the desert for a while. Sort of like the wilderness experience of Jesus, whose hairstyle he emulated. As a guitar player, feedback was his fallback.

Although that Feedback Fascination soon became a common thing in rock guitar solos, early rock (say pre-Hendrix) still avoided feedback as an unpleasant mistake.

> I recently heard a delectable story about James from someone who said he "read it in a book" so he assumed it was true and, for the sake of a good story, I'll assume that too:
> Growing up in Detroit, James was known as "The Human Hood Ornament." His father apparently, was a race-car driver who would tie young James to the hood of his car wearing a football helmet.
> Do we wonder that he later became a pioneer of psychedelic guitar?

Sam Andrew was the other guitarist in the band and maybe the musical director. A quiet guy with a Veronica Lake hairstyle, his playing, unlike James's, was composed of notes and chords that fit the song.

And Dave Getz was the band's drummer. A personable, witty guy who had started out intending to be a serious painter, Dave had an ability to step outside of what the band's reputation had become and comment on it, sometimes humorously, always perceptively.

And then there was <u>Janis</u> – the boss.

> Though Janis would eventually outstrip the others in the band in the Fame department, at the time I met them it was definitely a band: Big Brother And The Holding Company.
> Janis was the newest addition to the band. But, after her performance created a stir at Monterey, she was certainly not a diffident newcomer anymore (if she ever had been diffident—hard to imagine).

She was throwing her weight around with the band. There were lively discussions about their arrangements between her and 3 of the other members. James Gurley hardly entered these discussions. He was typically reserved.

Her presence took over the room. She wasn't very large, maybe 5'5" or so in my memory, but she seemed unable to sit quietly and just let things happen. She had an opinion and she was going to tell you what it was.
I noticed that she coated her outside with patchouli and her inside with Southern Comfort.

Since I'm basically a musician, I focused on her only on a professional, musical level. But otherwise she couldn't help but command my attention.

Non-conforming, smart, loud, brash, volatile, more sensitive than she appeared and the center of whatever storm was in progress.

All of those traits and more came out in the rehearsals but there was something else about the phenomenon of Janis Joplin that seemed to me even more significant.

She was a trailblazer and became a trend-setter. I think part of her vast popularity came in part from her appearance and the way she behaved.

Nowadays, rational and compassionate people are aware of the objectification of women and work to dispel it. But not in 1967.

Before Janis came on the scene "girl singers" looked and behaved a certain way. Look at pictures of Leslie Gore, Mary Wells and all the girls groups of the time. They look like their mother chose their outfits and did their hair.

Then take a look at Janis. Her mother didn't pick her outfit or do her hair.

Those were the years of Liberation. Beauty IS in the eye of the beholder but I've always thought that Janis was a symbol of liberation for every "plain girl" who had about given up trying to look like those gussied-up, coiffured young singers of the time.

For those young women, her sudden, enormous, universal popularity seemed to be like a violent eruption blasting out from their cosmetic frustration: "Yay! Now we've got a champion!"

There often seemed to be a clutch of women around her who seemed to be attendants to their champion, Queen Janis.

Their hippie costumes made them look like amateur actresses playing pioneer grandmothers in some community theater where there wasn't much of a costume budget.

But they were much too young to play grandmothers in their ratty shawls, handmade rustic dresses, beat-up sandals and complete obeisance to their bellowing, rough and raw mistress.

Janis's attendants

After that first rehearsal Albert and I planned to hear the band play live. They had a reputation for inspiring a level of excitement in their audience that was as much a part of their show as was their performance. In order to capitalize on that excitement they were eager to record a live album. So that was decided: this new album would be a live recording.

> The band was enthusiastic about that prospect. But I wasn't sure they had what it took to make a live recording. In a concert, mistakes are forgotten seconds after they occur but, on a record, MISTAKES LIVE FOREVER.

So we set up to record a live show at the Winterland Ballroom in San Francisco. It was called that because it had once been a skating rink.

Though the band may not have known it, this recording was, for Albert and me, an audition. Were they good enough for a live album?

My suspicions were confirmed. They played with an avalanche of energy and the screaming audience loved it but there were mistakes a-plenty so I knew we'd have to record in the studio where we could stop and start again to correct mistakes.

But word had already spread and already a <u>live</u> recording of Big Brother And The Holding Company was enthusiastically expected. I didn't want their fans to be disappointed.
Uh-oh. What to do?

I decided to <u>fake</u> a live recording. I'd done it before.

In 1965 Columbia had bought the original tapes of the Army-McCarthy hearings, in which fanatic senator Joseph McCarthy accused the army of harboring Communists, the number of which would change daily. The hearings were aired on TV in front of rapt viewers but they were, of course, monaural. I had to fake a live stereo recording of the proceedings for an album called "Point Of Order". I put the Army on the left and McCarthy, of course, on the right.

So I'd already gotten my fake-live feet wet.

But we were months away from making "Cheap Thrills". I had some other projects on my schedule first.

TRACK 23 — GORDY

People around him called him "Gordy". I never called him that. Whenever I wrote his name in my notes it would simply be four letters: LTFT, the articulated consonants of "Lightfoot.

Gordon Lightfoot was the first artist in Albert's stable that I took into the studio. He is a great singer and songwriter.

He told me that sometimes when he needs inspiration for a new group of songs he'll go to a strange town and walk the streets just looking at people and imagining what their stories might be.

For our recording sessions there were two Canadian musicians and two Americans. The two Canadians were his travelling band: John Stockfish on bass and guitarist, Red Shea. They were both amiable chaps. John was a fresh-faced youth and Red had the aura of someone who had been behind bars. Who knows if he ever <u>had</u> been but he looked like he might have been.

The two Americans were NYC studio pros: drummer Herbie Lovell and guitarist Hugh McCracken.

Herbie was a fine, left-handed drummer from New Orleans. I don't know how many times he had to switch his drums around after a studio engineer had set them up for a righty.

Hughie was a familiar face in the studios too, playing either guitar or harmonica.

> He could be a trickster too. Years later I went to a post-Katrina benefit concert in which Dr. John played. Hughie was in Dr. John's band. After the show I went backstage with some friends to say hello to Mac (Dr. John's given name). I saw Hughie standing guard outside of Mac's dressing room door keeping a cluster of fans at bay. I asked him if it was all right for us to go in. He said, "Sure, go right on in. This is a perfect time." We barged in and there was a surprised Mac in his skivvies.

For LTFT's album, I recorded once again on familiar grounds, Studio A at 799 7th Ave. which, since Columbia had been moved to new corporate headquarters, was now owned by A&R Studios, the recording home of famed producer and friend, Phil Ramone.

I wanted to add strings and horns to the basic recordings we'd done with Gordy and the rhythm section but, as the date for the sweetening session drew near, I came down with a fever that left me just short of delirious. Even so, I still had quite a few arrangements to write for the date.

I won't toot my own horn here; I'll let Lightfoot toot it for me. Here are the liner notes he wrote for that album:

> *"I first encountered John Simon in Philadelphia and he had a lot of ideas of his own. So he came up to Toronto a time later and we shot down each other's ideas for a couple of days. A week later we were getting the tracks down and everything sounded right when all of a sudden he pulls out this violin section. I couldn't believe it at first – well, I mean it sounded so fine altogether. So I just had to sit back and listen for awhile."*

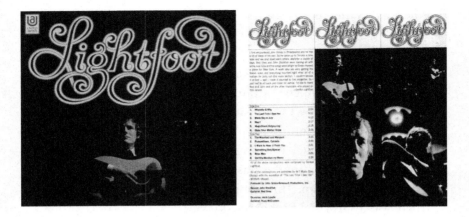

I'm real proud of the string parts I wrote for that album called "Did She Mention My Name". Matter of fact, they led to a mystery. A producer who was active in the advertising jingle business called me in for an interview.

I was excited because every composer in New York City knew that writing jingles could be a treasure trove that would lead to a yacht in the Mediterranean, a ski lodge in Biarritz and oodles of money to lose at the race track. And I was dying to make that connection and break into that very closed shop.

This advertising producer said to me, "Someone recommended your string writing to me very highly."
In my mind I was saying, "Who? Who? Who?"
And out of my mouth came, "Who? Who? Who?"

He never told me and I never knew, knew, knew. Never got to write a single jingle, jingle, jingle. Never got that yacht nor the ski lodge but I do go to the Saratoga racetrack every so often and manage to lose some money.

TRACK 24 – A PLACE CALLED WOODSTOCK

You may recall my meeting Peter Yarrow in United Airlines' First Class Lounge in the San Francisco airport. Now we were to start work in Woodstock on his movie project. I had never been there.

He said, "Meet me at the Café Espresso" (known locally as The Depresso). "But first, we've gotta get you a room."

My first night in Woodstock, I looked out from the gable window of a small motel on Route 375 (recently renamed "Levon Helm Boulevard" in gratitude for the commerce he brought to the town).

Even today when I drive past, I can't help but look to the left and pay some kind of silent homage to that window and how it opened a new chapter in my life.

The town of Woodstock has always had a distinct personality. It's not really a carbon copy of any other place. And the town's character had gone through changes over time before I saw it in 1967.

Late in the 18th century a grizzled bunch of loggers looked at the side of a mountain 100 miles north of New York City and may have said, "There's a pretty good <u>stock</u> of <u>wood</u> here."

Then, around the turn of the century (the turn before the last turn), a wealthy Englishman named Ralph Whitehead, inspired by the idealistic art critic John Ruskin, moved to America and tried to start a utopian community in a few different places. After failing with his first few tries, he finally settled on this mountainous locale in New York's Hudson Valley and, with 2 partners, created a refuge for artists and his free-thinking wacky friends. The artists who showed up then were almost indistinguishable from the hippies of 60 years later.

By the 1950s Woodstock was well-established as an art colony and the summer home of NYC's Arts Students League. A young painter named Vera would go there in the summers to be in the company of other artists and to be inspired by the lovely vistas of the Catskill Mountains.

Accompanying Vera was her son, young Peter Yarrow.

Fast-Forward to 1963.
Peter was then the first P of P,P&M and their manager was Albert Grossman, presently living in Chicago.

Albert was looking for a place close to NYC to live and Peter recommended the Woodstock of his childhood. Albert bought a house there and soon took on the management of a young folk-singer named Bob Dylan.

Bob, from Minnesota, had been crashing here and there in NYC and decided that he too would move to Woodstock.

And that was the scene when I arrived in 1967.

I wasn't in that motel room for long. Peter rented a house where I would stay and where filmmaker Howard Alk and I would assemble Peter's movie.

The movie, "You Are What You Eat", started out as a documentary on the Hells Angels but 1967's Summer Of Love got in the way and the camera shifted from bikers to hippies and the filmmakers shifted from the coffee pot to just plain pot. And LSD.

The result was a stack of 16mm film cans with no apparent order and it was Howard's job and my job to make a movie out of all of that.

Howard and friend.

Howard was brilliant at it. He had a great sense of humor. Physically, he was more bear than human with a big laugh and a bigger intellect. He had been part of Chicago's Second City troupe and a friend of Albert's in the Second City.

He came East and was a welcomed fixture alongside Bob Dylan and on Dylan's tour.

Howard found ways to tie segments of "You Are What You Eat" together so that the connections <u>seemed</u> intentional, though they weren't.

Part of my job was to look for the same kind of connections and try to come up with song possibilities at the same time.

There was some footage of a Haight-Ashbury crash pad called The Greta Garbo Home for Wayward Boys and Girls. I looked at all of it and I noticed this kid running through a lot of the shots. About three years old, dressed in a shapeless sack his hippie mom may have stitched for him before cooking wild rice and buckwheat groats for 15 or 20 stoners. The residents of the Greta Garbo Home were a wild bunch: on good trips, bad trips, crazy hair, tie-dye, body paint, clouds of smoke, free love. But to this kid it all seemed normal. What did <u>he</u> know after all. He was <u>three</u>!

So I wrote an innocent little happy song from what I supposed might be the point-of-view of the innocent little happy kid I saw through the movieola.

> *My name is Jack*
> *And I live in the back*
> *Of the Greta Garbo Home*
> *With friends I will remember*
> *Wherever I may roam…*

(1967)

Somehow Manfred Mann heard it and, after recording "The Mighty Quinn", he recorded the song and it still gets played today... Mostly in Germany because the Germans think Manfred Mann is German. (He's actually from South Africa.)

One night while Howard and I were busily trying to make a movie out of those cans of film, there was this god-awful bleating outside. We went to the window and there were four guys dressed in a halfhearted gesture toward Halloween playing instruments with which they apparently were unfamiliar, serenading Howard because, I think, it was his birthday.

Those four guys plus one more would eventually become known as The Band.

What were they doing in Woodstock?
Well, the story has been written so many times I shudder to tell it. But shudder I will and here goes, as I heard it.

When Bob Dylan was looking for a backup band, Mary Martin, a bright dynamic employee of Albert's, suggested a group from her native Canada who had recently been the band of Ronnie Hawkins, rockabilly performer from Arkansas.

(L-R)Richard, Rick, Levon, Ronnie, Robbie, Garth

Little by little, most of them became the nucleus of Bob's backup band.

Then Bob had a motorcycle accident and his performing had to stop. But he kept the band on salary and lodged them in a house he rented near Woodstock.

During his recuperation, Bob and the guys would get together to have fun and make music. Some of that was later released and "monetized" (a word I absolutely hate) as "The Basement Tapes".

(As Ron Carter, bass player non-pareil, said to me, "There's a reason they're called outtakes.")

At that point it was common knowledge around Woodstock that Bob's back-up band was itching to make an album of their own.

Howard Alk had heard my zany Marshall McLuhan album and he had heard a tape that Robbie, Richard, Rick and Garth had recorded in that very basement—another tape beside what has come to be known as "The Basement Tapes". It was entitled "Even If It's a Pig, Part Two". Like the McLuhan album, it was a crackpot production. So Howard thought that we all would be a good match.

He was right.

TRACK 25 – BIG PINK

After that residence in Woodstock working on "You Are What You Eat", I returned to NYC and the phone rang. It was Robbie Robertson.

Back when I was breaking in as a producer at Columbia, I co-produced an album along with veteran jazz producer George Avakian by tenor sax player Charles Lloyd, featuring Tony Williams, Ron Carter and Hungarian guitarist Gabor Szabo. Charles and Robbie knew each other slightly (I think they shared the same pot connection.) and Charles had invited Robbie to join his band in the studio for a song or two. That's when we first met.

Then, two years later, there was Howard Alk's birthday serenade.

Robbie's call told me what I already knew: that he and the other guys in Dylan's backup band were hoping to make a record and they needed a producer.

They had been in the studio with producers before. I heard that producer/arranger Henry Glover had been in charge of some early Ronnie Hawkins sessions. And there was a wisp of information floating around that Motown producer, Mickey Stevenson had taken a shot at recording them. But I'm not certain of that.

Robbie invited me back up to Woodstock to talk about going into the studio. So back to Woodstock I went.

He took me directly to Big Pink, the ordinary little pink house that Dylan had rented for them. Garth Hudson, Rick Danko and Richard Manuel were living there and, as Robbie and I drove up, Levon Helm and his friend, Kirby Penick came walking out of the woods.

With a handshake and a warm Southern greeting, Levon seemed happier than a pig in shit after his walk through the forest neighborhood. It had to be a lot more bucolic than his most recent surroundings: working on an oil rig off the Louisiana coast with Kirby.

> Levon had not been part of the band that backed Bob on his recent world tour because, as he put it, he didn't like being part of a band that Bob's die-hard Folkie Fans were booing every night (pretty violent for peaceniks, ironically).
> They booed because they felt betrayed. Bob was leaving folk music behind for the more vivid palette of rock and roll. "He's gone electric", they despairingly moaned.
> I believe Mickey Jones was the drummer for that tour.

So, if you've put two and two together, you've figured out that, contrary to the rewriting of rock history, Levon was <u>not</u> there for those celebrated "basement tapes" recordings. Richard was the principal drummer.

> (Levon was not shy about world travel though. A few years later, at the advent of their new popularity as The Band, Levon told me that he was looking forward to "seeing the world from a drum stool".)

In the time that the guys spent incubating their music at Big Pink, Robbie, in Levon's absence (and considering the easy-going, deferential nature of the 3 other remaining members) had clearly become the leader of the group.
He proved to be a canny individual (and he has been consistent in that respect since I've known him). While he was checking me out as a potential partner in the upcoming escapade, he told me about the music they were making but he didn't let me hear the tapes. It wasn't until two trips

later that he was going to let me hear the demos that he and the others had recorded on an old reel-to-reel tape machine in the basement of Big Pink.

The guys had set up their studio just inside that basement garage door.

So I sat by the furnace in that cramped makeshift basement studio and listened.

I loved what I heard. Sure it was crude, but it wasn't a copy-cat derivative of anything I knew.

> The playing was unique: Garth was all over the place, many levels above the organists and pianists in other rock groups.
> Rick played the bass melodically. They weren't just oom-pah bass parts.
> Richard was hearing things that other rock drummers wouldn't even consider that came out in his fearless drumming.
> Robbie's tremulous solos and his rhythm patterns were all perfectly well-chosen.
> And the voices! Rick and Richard could howl like in-tune wolves or gentle along a sweet melody.

That was what I heard in their music. And, in talking with them, I realized quickly that these guys were different from other artists I'd worked with.

They had a deep respect, bordering on reverence, for the roots of American music, stretching back from the music of their generation, through rock-abilly and early rock and roll, to the Bluegrass of Appalachia, the Blues of the Mississippi Delta and even Stephen Foster and popular music of the 19th Century.

And it seemed to me that they had a sort of unspoken commitment to be as good as they could in order to earn their place as part of that tradition.

(L-R:) Rick, Levon, Richard, Garth (holding a divining rod), Robbie.

(George Harrison once told them,
"You all will have no trouble aging. You look old already.)

Some of the songs I heard came from Bob's fertile imagination. Some were collaborations and some were exclusively Robbie's creations. Robbie had obviously learned a lot from being in such close proximity to Bob, particularly in the story songs and the freewheeling imagery. But he had been more open than Bob to exploring many different types of music, so that the chords and structure of the new songs he was writing tended to be more adventurous than Bob's folk music sources. And there was humor in them (I love humor.).

But now, with the band embarking on its own, Robbie would fill the song-writing gap left by Bob's separation from their basement workshop.

How would he know how he was doing?

Robbie told critic Ralph J. Gleason in a Rolling Stone article that, for The Band recordings, "John Simon was that outside ear and outside opinion you could trust."

Often, in the bubbling pot of a long project, I wasn't always sure that everything I was doing was helping to move things along. So I'm pleased and proud that he said that.

So I was in. I was living alone again so it was easy for me to crash just about anywhere.

Woodstock at the time was a sort of safe haven for music stars at all levels of fame. It wasn't like Hollywood with its Maps To The Homes Of The Stars or Nashville with its Country Music Hall Of Fame. The local population was made up of a few small farms, tradespeople and folks who made the 20 minute commute to the mammoth IBM complex in Kingston. The Famous could walk the streets like The Not-So-Famous. I'd see John Sebastian at Houst's Hardware, Maria Muldaur at the library, Bob Dylan at Mower's Market.

One day I was taking a nap on the couch and there was a knock at the door. It was Bob.

"Come in, Bob."

He asked me if I'd be his Musical Secretary for a film score he was doing. I thought I could probably make better use of my time than to scribble down whatever fragments of melody occurred to him. That was probably a bad decision because it would've been cool just to hang around with such a special person. But I declined.

I would rehearse and work on the arrangements with the guys during the day and later we'd all grab a table at Deanie's restaurant where 60-year-old Flo Shultis, stone-faced in her pancake make-up and jewels, would crank out unembellished piano stylings of Gershwin and Cole Porter melodies at the spinet.

The guys had no early-to-bed-early-to-rise obligations like their IBM neighbors so they rattled around town eccentrically, getting into generally harmless mishaps on a regular basis. Richard liked to drink, and they all smoked a lot of pot so there might be "incidents", like the night of the "drive-in".

Richard had brushed his rent-a-car against a guardrail and it got stuck there. When Levon heard about it, he heroically rushed to the scene to come to the aid of his bandmate. But he wheeled around the curb a little too quickly and smashed his fiberglass Corvette into the local police car that was already on the scene. It turned to powder. Later that night, probably in my subconscious zeal to be included in this drama, I backed my car into a tree.

(Richard was so hard on cars, when he would show up at the Hertz office in Kingston for a new vehicle, Lou, the manager, would hide.)

So Fate had brought the 6 of us together back in 1967 and we worked very closely together for about 3 years.

There they were and there I was.
In the right place at the right time.

What was my role in the process of making records as the "new guy" with this band that had been playing together for years? They brought their talents to the project of recording an album and I, like each of them, brought mine. What did I add at that point?

Well, it didn't feel like producing a record had felt to me before. I felt like I was contributing as an equal partner with the members of the band, sometimes discussing the songs themselves with Robbie, but mostly attending to the arrangements.

Working with The Band, was it a democracy? Pretty much. Nothing went on those records that each of us didn't approve of.

I felt for the first time that I was in a sort of lab without the pressure of a record company demanding a finished album by a certain date. We were experimenting with music song-by-song with no clear idea of the result, just seeing where those experiments might take us.

For me it was some kinda Heaven, both musically and person-
ally. The richness of it. Intoxicating. (Of course the marijuana
didn't dispel my euphoria.)

I was happy there. I wanted to stay. One day I asked Robbie if I
could join up. He said, "We've already got two piano players."

And that was that.

Finally, when we felt we'd rehearsed enough material to make a demo for
Albert to peddle, I took the guys into the studio with which I was most
familiar: Columbia's old Studio A.

> When we got to the studio, engineer Don Hahn had set up the
> session as he would ordinarily have done, with sound barriers
> between the instruments.
>
> But we had been rehearsing in a small space where everyone
> could pretty much reach out and touch each other.
>
> After doing a little sound-check, we realized that wasn't going to
> work. The guys were accustomed to playing in close proximity
> to each other in the basement. So we put those baffles away and
> re-grouped "in the open".
>
> Besides, they didn't need the protection of separation, in which,
> if someone made a mistake, that mistake wouldn't "bleed" into
> the other microphones.
>
> They didn't make mistakes.

In one afternoon we recorded fully a third of the album that was to
become Big Pink: "Tears of Rage", "We Can Talk about It Now", "Chest
Fever", "This Wheel's On Fire" and "The Weight".

> Although I can't remember for sure the sequence of the record-
> ings, I do remember the spirit of it all and, if I don't get this
> exactly right, it'll be real close.

"Tears of Rage" had become sort of a test case in my mind. If we could
get this song's potential on tape, then the rest would follow. The beautiful

lyrics were written by Dylan and Richard wrote the tune that he himself would sing.

During rehearsals, Robbie had been fooling around with a weathered box that had a Leslie speaker inside that we simply called "the black box". The sound of the guitar through it seemed right for this song. Robbie had a sort of fanfare phrase in mind as an intro.

I imagined an eccentric syncopated accent for the rhythm section to play under Robbie's opening lick and throughout the verses of the song.

Later, Robbie told me that Eric Clapton had a hard time "getting" that particular rhythm phrasing.

Garth was intrigued because I had played a baritone horn in high school, which I never thought I'd play again. He worked up a moaning horn lick for us to play between the verses.

With Rick's melodic bass lines and Levon's drumming on instruments that were intentionally "tubby" and not crisp like most rock and roll drums, we knew we were getting somewhere.

We had changed the key of the song to get the most out of Richard's voice. While Dylan's vocal on the basement demo was certainly pained, Richard was, as all would admit, more of a singer. There seemed to be real tears behind his deeply-felt vocal. In the choruses, Rick added a high harmony part, but it wasn't a tight harmony in lock-step to Richard's phrasing; he sang with his own personal expression, phrasing it on his own.

After that, for the drama, I overdubbed tambourine rolls in the chorus. Even though playing the baritone horn was fun and added a lot to the mood of the song, I was even happier that the idea of that funereal tambourine and drum part occurred to me.

Afterwards, listening back on the soft sofas in the control room, we all couldn't have been happier. All the elements were there just as we'd rehearsed them but now they'd been frozen in time with the crystalline sound of a professional recording studio.

We were on a roll and eager to keep going. Next we tried "We Can Talk About It Now", written by Richard, which had become another of my favorites.

> When Levon rejoined the band at Big Pink, we had to fold his voice into the vocal parts that had already been split up between Rick and Richard. "We Can Talk About It Now" was a good opportunity to do that. It was worked out that the 3 of them would divide up the vocals, each totally independent and personal in his phrasing. It was like a free-form hacky-sack session where they'd just lob the sack back and forth playfully.
>
> When we were working out the arrangements for the songs, we never took it for granted that the same groove would remain when a new section came up. So for the bridge (what the Brits call "The Middle Eight"), we decided to abandon the straight 8th-note feel and lope into a shuffle under Richard's vocal instead.

We didn't want to break for lunch. We wanted to keep going. So in came the pizzas and we continued with "Chest Fever" which became a standard during all subsequent live shows by The Band.

> Garth sat down at his Lowrey organ. This would be a spot for him to show his stuff. The Lowrey had a button he could push with the side of his foot in order to slide the pitch down one note. That's how he could get a sound sort of like a steel guitar at times. His uncle, apparently, was an undertaker and Garth, as a youngster, played the organ for memorial services. But the breadth of his musical interests was enormous.

He began an intro that was a gesture toward a Bach Toccata and Fugue before launching into plain-old rock 'n roll. In came the drums and we were off and running.

(Levon told me he thought Garth's contributions made the band "The Band". I wouldn't go that far – there was more that set them apart from other groups, but Garth certainly contributed to their recognizable gestalt.)

I had felt that the guys' original arrangement of "Chest Fever" might be improved and we rehearsed it and recorded it with my changes. However, when they later played it on the road, they were so comfortable with the old way of doing it that they went back to their original arrangement.

Because only Garth read music, sometimes I'd become a living page of music paper for the others – signaling the guys when a new section was coming up. That was really the case with Levon. On "Chest Fever" and countless times while we were recording, I'd lean on the baffles in front of the drums and point to different drums or cymbals to help him remember what was coming up next, like the bridge on this particular song. My conducting him that way was a help in taking that concern off his mind so that he could simply get into the music. It was a good arrangement (in both senses of the word).

The invocation of The Salvation Army in the bridge is pretty wacky. But it does serve the function of lifting the song from being "just" rock 'n roll.

Then on to "This Wheel's On Fire", written by Rick to Dylan's words.

As Rick sang in his quivering tenor, the song's downright eerie diminished chords reminded me again of Halloween, just like when I'd first heard it at Big Pink.

Garth played the clavinet through some kind of weird effect. Even in 1967, he was already hungry for the sonic possibilities of new sound gear.

But by now we were beginning to show Studio Fatigue. Donny Hahn and I goofed. We recorded Levon's snare drum too softly.

As much as working in rock music had become my job, I was still a jazz head. The way I hear it, in jazz the high-hat provides the focus of the rhythm for the players. But in rock and roll it's the snare. In the words of Chuck Berry,

"Rock and roll music, Any old way you choose it; It's got a back beat, you can't lose it".

("Rock and Roll Music", Chuck Berry, 1957)

We realized this too late and we knew Levon would have to overdub the snare drum. He wasn't happy about that and I don't blame him. He sighed and said, "Never ask me to do that again." And I never had to.

After that, I thought we were through. We'd put in a long day and, after weeks of preparation, we'd really accomplished what we'd set out to do. Those carefully thought-out arrangements, the energetic vocals and perfectly played instrumental parts. There they were on tape, forever. Whew!

But then Robbie pulled out an acoustic guitar which I hadn't seen him play at all during our days rehearsing at Big Pink.

I thought, "What's up?"
So I said, "What's up?"

It turned out that he and Levon had been working on "The Weight" as an opportunity for Levon to sing a lead vocal.

The arrangement came together in the studio. Garth and Richard switched seats.

Before Richard had joined Ronnie Hawkins he had been exclusively a vocalist. But Ronnie didn't want anyone else in his band standing up with a microphone and no instrument. So Richard, a quick study, learned to play the piano. He said to me once, "Y'know how some bands have a lead guitar and a rhythm guitar? Well, I play rhythm piano."

Using that analogy, Garth played lead piano. He had plenty of chops to play the filigree fills in the choruses of "The Weight".

Levon sang the lead from his drum stool, except for one particularly light-humored verse that Robbie assigned to Rick.

Over time, The Weight" has become the song most associated with The Band over all the others.

What made it a hit?

Well, it had a lot going for it: a vivid, sad and wistful story, a simple, repeated chorus with the clever hook of a staggered vocal line at the end, easy chords for any guitar-playing fan to learn, a noble homeless hero, his off-camera sweetheart, humor and, except for the one whimsical verse that Rick sang, the plaintive, geographically-authentic voice of Levon Helm.

> "I pulled into Nazareth. I was feeling 'bout half past dead..."
> (The Weight, J.R. Robertson, 1968)

It's chemistry.

That was it. We finished an epic day in the studio and packed up.

The next day I started playing the rough tapes from the session for our friends. In Albert's NYC office I heard congratulations from Bobby

Neuwirth, Howard Alk and Howard's wife, Jonesy. And Albert got so much confirmation as to the quality of the stuff from people he trusted that he probably felt confident flying with a tape to LA.

He got us a deal.
With Capitol Records.
We were to fly out to LA to finish the album there, which was an excellent idea because winter was coming on in Woodstock and the prospect of Southern California sun seemed irresistible.

TRACK 26 – THE ONLY ONE
WHO WAS THERE

So we went out to LA, checked into the Château Marmont hotel and showed up for our first session at Capitol's renowned studios at Hollywood and Vine.

The staff engineer assigned to us was a lanky, taciturn, pipe-smoking, Gary Cooper look-alike named Rex Updegraft.

> (It seemed like a lot of people in Hollywood were look-alikes for one movie star or another.)

We got the feel of the room and played what we'd recorded in New York for Rex. I'll never forget his comment when we asked him what he thought of our music. Rex said, "Darned cute."

Well, we probably could've finished up the album there in a couple of days but instead we stayed out of the studio for awhile. I suppose Capitol thought we were rehearsing or writing, but we had just left a Woodstock winter and were just basking in the California sun, having a good time and keeping warm. It would be almost a month before we'd go back into the Capitol studio a second time.

> One day, Levon and I decided to satisfy our curiosity about something brand-new. We asked the other guys but we were the only two brave enough to walk from the Chateau Marmont next door to the Imperial Gardens restaurant to try this new scary food we'd heard about: raw fish
> From then on, he always loved sushi.

Eventually, with the advent of spring and tolerable weather back east, we knew we could return to a warmer Woodstock so we decided we'd better get back to work and went back into the studio. Studios had a generic, uniform look about them back then: very business-like with no frills. You wouldn't find posters of rock stars on the walls, nor colored lights for atmosphere. Being in a studio gave you no clue as to your actual longitude and latitude. It was the same as being on the road and going through one airport after another without really knowing what city you're in.

We set up as we did in Studio A in NYC with a minimum of baffles separating the players. We'd become influenced by the California mellow vibe by then. So, in that mood, we started off with a ballad, "Lonesome Suzie", a beauty, which is pure Richard.

> He wrote it and sang it. The words laid out a wistful portrait but, sitting there in the studio, I once again noticed how the melody and chords were indebted to black gospel music. Garth could play comfortably in that genre. Adjusting the organ's stops throughout the takes, he showed what a master of sound qualities he is. Robbie played some soulful guitar fills while Richard sang an absolutely beautiful vocal.

We'd all fallen in love with the sound of our unconventional "horn section" (Garth and me) and their moaning parts seemed perfect for the song so we added them as well.

And the result? Ahhh! Some euphoric place beyond "darned cute".

Since we were set up for Richard to sing the lead, we tried another of the songs he wrote, "In A Station".

The musical texture of that song was intended to be less gospel-y and more dream-like. Garth rigged up one of his sound-contraptions that was basically a Rocksichord.

We overdubbed Levon and Rick singing some parts that weren't typical Band vocals. The long notes they sang were like conventional "background vocal" parts. But we didn't follow the conventions of singing "Ooo" or "Ahh". We hand-tooled them. For instance, when Levon and Rick echoed Richard singing "Once upon a time leaves me empty", they let their answer sort of melt away: "Once upon a time leaves me em—".

There was no doubt that we had fallen under that laid-back Southern California spell. So the next day in the studio, we purposefully picked up the tempo and recorded one of Robbie's earlier songs, "Caledonia Mission".

This time Rick sang the melody and Richard sang the high harmonies.

I was happy to get a chance to play the piano on this song. Robbie nursed me through what he wanted my part to sound like.

(I have to note here that whenever I got a chance to play on a record, this or any other, it required a different mindset.

There's something somewhat leisurely about being a producer: you have the objectivity to just sit back, relax, listen and comment. But, as a player, you've got to be more on your toes. What you're playing will be captured forever so you'd better do the very best you can.)

One of the best songs that came out of the Big Pink basement was "I Shall Be Released". It was 100% Dylan.

> Those songs that Bob wrote in Woodstock seemed to lack the violence, the hard edge of his earlier "city" songs about war, murder, assassination, etc. Now he was in the rural tranquility of country life, enjoying the privilege of isolation from urban angst, sort of like living in Versailles prior to the French Revolution.

People often characterize Bob's songs as having cutting-edge or off-the-wall lyrics. But there's something else about them: they're catchy. They have "hooks". Because of that, "I Shall Be Released" became a campfire favorite in the Sixties.

> This was an opportunity to use the terrific blend of the 3 voices that we had available. They gave Robbie as a songwriter a rich vocal palette to utilize. As I've said elsewhere, his use of the guys' individual distinctive vocal qualities reminds me of Duke Ellington's use of the special colors of his horn soloists.

> Rick would sing in his beautifully clear, often vibrato-less tone, pitch-perfect, poetic and poignant. Richard could sound like Ray Charles or sing in a high falsetto that would have sounded like a squeak if it didn't have so much soul in it. And Levon, with his authentic Delta inflection, had a voice like beautiful dirt. (That's an odd description but somehow it seems pretty good.)

> For "I Shall Be Released" Richard sang the falsetto lead with Rick in the middle and Levon on the bottom in the choruses.

> There was something poignant about the song that reminded me in a crazy subjective way of a military funeral. So, for the

snare drum sound, I was hearing something vaguely martial in my head and I suggested to Levon that he flip his snare over and run his finger across the actual metal snares for the back beat. It seemed to fit. He liked the idea and it worked out fine.

When we had cut our "demo" back in Studio A, we were pressed for time (and money). But, now that we had our deal, we could spend several days in the studio rather than just a few hours. So we tried lots of songs, most of which didn't make it onto the eventual album. Many of them were silly throw-aways but it was a luxury to have the time booked to get our studio chops together.

As he had done in Studio A in New York with "The Weight", Robbie pulled out another surprise song to try.

"Long Black Veil" is a country song whose lyrics by Maryjohn Wilkin fit beautifully into the backwoods, spooky story-telling that nuanced a lot of the songs we were recording. It's got a great story that develops carefully over the verses.

> There was something relaxing about recording "Long Black Veil". The original songs that we'd been doing were still untested. So there was a little bit of subconscious anxiety about how they'd be received. But "Long Black Veil", so well written, was already a solid success, so we could confidently lean on that.

> Rick spun out the sad tale in a plaintive vocal and Richard and Levon joined in for the choruses.
> I was recruited to hit some real low notes on the baritone horn, adding a touch of doom.

There was one other song from the Capitol sessions that made it onto the eventual album: "To Kingdom Come".

> When Robbie wrote a song he would usually sing it to whomever was going to sing it on the record. And in doing so, the singer

couldn't help but pick up a lot of Robbie's inflections in the vocal melodies. But, with three great singers in the band, there wasn't any need for him to sing.

The result was interesting. The singers were stand-ins for Robbie. They sang with the phrasing he would've used if he were as good at it as they were.

But there came a point in the studio, maybe at the urging of the others, when Robbie got over his feeling of comparative vocal inadequacy and it was decided that his voice would get onto the album. "To Kingdom Come" would be the chance for that to happen.

When he got in front of the vocal mike, he was sheepish and tentative. He wasn't sure his vocal was good enough. So, on the first verse, Richard sang along with him, doubling the melody: *"Forefather pointed to Kingdom Come, sadly told his only son, 'Just be careful what you do. It all comes back on you.'"*. But, in the corresponding spot in the 2nd verse, he sang the lines all alone: *"We've been sittin' in here for so darn long…"*
Rick sang the second section of each verse and then Richard, Rick and Levon sang the choruses together.

At the end of the recording, Robbie played a nice long guitar solo, aerated with welcome pauses, showing off his moaning style, bending strings and plucking harmonics.

We finished in LA and went back to Springtime in New York to mix the album. The mixing engineer was a fine, musical gentleman named Tony May who taught me a lot about mixing and with whom I had the pleasure of working many times over the years. The place we mixed? You guessed it: the old Columbia mixing rooms, now owned by A&R.

(I should say here that this was the first time I worked on an album that racked up hundreds of hours of studio time. Simon

and Garfunkel had shaken up the 4-songs-in-3-hours proto-
type for me that had been the previous recording studio norm.
But, having been busy with other projects and not completing
"Bookends" with them, I had no experience in the kind of studio
immersion that working with The Band would afford.

Consequently, when someone asked me why I don't have as
many rich stories about other artists—like Gordon Lightfoot or
Leonard Cohen, for instance—my answer was that I didn't spend
as much time in the studio with them!)

When it was time to put the record out, the band still had no name. A
strong contender was "The Crackers". There was even an old poster that
was being considered for the album cover. It displayed the labels of different types of crackers But in the end everyone in Woodstock knew the
guys as "the band" so that's what they became.

Bob Dylan contributed a painting for the cover, which looks like something that Marc Chagall might have painted if someone woke him up too
quickly from a nap.

The liner notes, brief as they were, were written by Dominique, Robbie's French-speaking, Canadian wife, which would help to explain the limping syntax.

And Elliott Landy, a photographer whose work had appeared in Rat Magazine, was chosen to take the band's picture.

For the photo shoot we went up to Rick's Uncle Lee's farm in Ontario.

In a gesture to their roots, the guys invited their families to be in the shot. Levon's folks couldn't make the trip up from Arkansas so they appear in the inset in the upper corner.

But here, for the edification of all, is that photograph with a key identifying who's who.

Then it became time to sequence the album.

Nowadays we often hear songs for the first time isolated, alone, not connected with other songs. But back in those Days-Before-Noah's-Flood, the product of one's studio labors was presented to listeners in a context, in sort of a story form. This was real important. People making records paid a lot of attention to the sequence of songs on an album. Most albums started with a bang and ended with a bang.

We knew we were making music that didn't conform to the norm, so when Robbie suggested opening with the slow "Tears Of Rage", it made sense. When people put the record on their turntable, they'd hear an opening they wouldn't expect.

This was some new shit.

The record, as a whole, was some new shit. After The Beatles, pop music was stalled in copy-cat repetition.

But, even though the General Populace was slow to catch on, "Music From Big Pink" was a gust of fresh air so strong that it was on every musician's turntable in 1968. And an entirely new strain of pop music was born that eventually came to be called "Americana".

Here's a first-hand account from Joe Boyd, producer of the British Band, Fairport Convention:

> *"As they pondered the future that spring, the record on all their turntables was Music from Big Pink by The Band. It had thrown down the gauntlet: You want to play American music? Well, try playing something as American as this! It was a revolutionary record: their schooling in the Southern roadhouses with Ronnie Hawkins followed by their work as Dylan's backing group meant they were at once both source and emulators. Fairport felt Big Pink meant that a return to their trademark style wasn't an option."*
> (from "White Bicycles: Making Music in the 1960s")

Pile up enough trivia and you get the whole story. There's a lot more of course but those are all the "Big Pink" memories that come to mind on this particular rainy February day over 50 years later, and it's the Truth as I remember it.

But there's plenty of Hearsay surrounding The Band as well. Here are a couple of choice examples, both concerning Rick:

#1:
John Kruth, a fine writer and adventurous musician, told me this one (which I have paraphrased):

He was the opening act for Rick in a small club in some remote corner of Canada like Moosenuts, Manitoba. This was long after The Band had broken up and Rick had gained a LOT of weight. After the gig, they hit an all-night diner to eat something. The joint was empty. The waitress approached.

Rick ordered a cheeseburger. Then another. Then another and another and another. And fries and more fries. And why don't you add a chicken to that.
And a couple of steaks. And mac and cheese. Make that 3 orders of mac and cheese. And a huge salad (gotta eat healthy) and a chocolate shake. Better make that a few of those and throw in the a couple more, but vanilla. Got any pizza?
John couldn't believe what he was hearing and when the food arrived there was no room left on the table; the platters spilled over onto the tables surrounding them.

But just then, a pile of fans from the show discovered Rick in the diner and, lo and behold, he had a banquet laid out for all of them.

That one I believe to be true because I trust the source.
The second…?

#2:
In a blog called "Rick Danko – The High Lonesome Voice of The Band, the blogger reports :

"Rick was known for many things, but punctuality was not one of them."
(Well, we'll skip that part though, in my experience, Rick was always the first to arrive at the recording studio eager to work.
The blogger is probably referring to his practice later in life.
But here's the kicker:)

"Rick was even late for Festival Express, the legendary train-based tour across Canada with The Band, the Dead, Janis... One account has John Simon driving the car alongside the train with Rick jumping out of the car from the passenger's side and running after the train..."

Wow! Whose account was THAT? In spite of wanting to perpetuate the picture of myself as a participant in a dashing, daring motorized caper, I have to reveal that I never even HEARD of the Festival Express until months after it happened.
Phew! Pure Hearsay!

Me NOT driving Rick to catch The Festival Express.

My association with these guys was one of the most exciting, most fun, most creative, freeest periods of my life.

For what it's worth (and to me it's worth a lot) I was the only one who was there for every minute, every note of the first two albums.

That's saying something.

TRACK 27 — "CHEAP THRILLS"

Working on "Music From Big Pink" had been a heady experience. The musical palette was so broad and so deep. We really got into the arrangements and the guys had the ability to be instrumentally adventurous and hold onto rock-solid rhythm at the same time. There were 3 excellent, unique singers. And the song material was a great foundation to build on.

Also the guys in The Band accepted the hard work necessary to get everything right. They were serious about making a fine record. And they had been together for so long that they already had a cohesion that other groups would take years to achieve. They were also a lot of fun to hang out with.

In my mind they were a hard act to follow. I felt sorry for whatever band I would be assigned to assist next.

That next band was to be Big Brother And The Holding Company.

> On one coast, in laid-back California, Capitol was in no hurry to release Music From Big Pink because there had been no publicity about The Band. Nobody knew who they were yet. Capitol didn't know what they had.

> On the other hand, Columbia, on the East Coast, was chomping at the bit in its eagerness to get the Big Brother album out in light of the publicity surrounding Janis and the Monterey performance.

Now Columbia's wait was over. I'd finished with The Band's album and finally the time came to go into the studio with Big Brother.

I've got to say that my memories of those recording dates aren't as clear as the Band sessions. I do remember certain episodes though.

The sessions were pretty haphazard, which wasn't exactly my style. The Haight-Ashbury <u>hippie</u> M.O. was "organic" and that sometimes meant random, unfocused, hardly goal-oriented. There was the danger of things spinning completely out of control.

At the same time, it was my responsibility to deliver a record album. But I had no Haight-Ashbury "street creds". I found myself without any leverage with the band. My skills were musical and organizational. The organizational part sure wasn't working. But I still had to rein them in.

I realized that I might be able to do that if I kept them concentrating on achieving a certain level of <u>musical</u> performance. And that I knew how to do.

The recording of George Gershwin's "Summertime" was a good example. For that song the guys wanted an intro that was like a Bach fugue but they didn't really know how to accomplish that. They got as far as imagining some contrapuntal, weaving melodies but they hadn't figured out how to make them work as pleasant harmonies at the same time.

Well! As a music major who'd gone through all the harmonizations in the Bach Chorale books, there was finally a way that I could be of some use, apart from generally trying to wrangle them.

So we began every session by rehearsing that intro. I'll lay it out here as simply as I laid it out to them:

Since the song is in the key of A minor, at the important downbeat of each measure each of them could try to play any one of the three notes in an A minor chord (A, C or E).

That was a help. And then I asked them to try the same thing in the middle of the bar.

We started every session rehearsing "Summertime" and after awhile, lo and behold, chaos was slowly turning into order and we rolled tape and got that intro.

Speaking of "Summertime", I have to give credit to Sam Andrew for a musical innovation. That song had been recorded countless times but I'd never heard any version with the subtle touch that Sam added.

It's hard to describe music in words but I'll try. See if you can follow this. Janis sings:

"*Summertime, time, time*" – then there's a chord.

It's on the downbeat of the second measure and it's a <u>diminished chord</u>. That was Sam's choice. And I'd never heard anyone else do it. It's fabulous.

While we were making the record, I became aware of was how much of a democracy the group was. Although Janis was the obvious blazing star, several numbers featured vocals by other band members. Of course that was true because she was the newcomer in the band. Before she had joined them, they already had some repertoire in place in which they sang leads. But even then, her voice as part of the background vocals eclipsed the lead vocal.

Although she was the newest addition to Big Brother, it was plain to see and to hear that Janis was the star. And as such she had become the leader.

>In a zenith of understatement her name is just listed in the corner of the *Cheap Thrills* album cover as "Janis Joplin, vocal."

"Cheap Thrills" is the album it is because of Janis, because of her raw emotion, her energy. She gave it her all. She was a blues shouter. Raw. She practiced.

She even practiced her screams. I remember her trying out different screams for us, saying, "This is the way Tina Turner would scream. Or I could do it like Big Mama Thornton."
I came from a jazz background and appreciated spontaneity and improvisation. I didn't think that planning spontaneous screams was sincere and I judged her harshly because of that. But, in retrospect, I realize she was just trying to do the best she could.

Among the songs she wanted to record was "Piece Of My Heart". I loved the original recording by Erma Franklin, Aretha's sister. So I was real happy Janis was going to do it. It was a perfect vehicle for her range of emotions. She could start off a verse almost whispering and then just about scream the chorus.

At first it was the big hit off the album although, over the years, "Summertime" is remembered more – for many, her recording of "Summertime" has become the definitive version of the song.

As a producer I would always seek the stamp of approval from the artist about everything that was going on the record, no matter who came up with the idea or performance. So it was Janis to whom I looked. I may have called the shots as to what we did next, whether we needed another take, what in my opinion was right and what was wrong. But it was Janis whose approval was necessary. And this wasn't always easy. Progress didn't always go in a straight line because of her wild-card drinking.

As it turns out this dynamic was pretty accurately recorded by Don Pennybaker in the film he shot of a recording session. While I was trying to push us toward accomplishing something or other, Janis was ignoring whatever our objective was at the time and was wrapped up in telling us all a story.

Because things were going so slowly, I was getting impatient and didn't really see any point in capturing all that frustration on film, cinema verite or not. I didn't think it would enhance Big Brother's career or boost record sales. So at one point I wheeled on Pennybaker and his camera and said, "Turn that fucking thing off!"

That was my film debut. (My mom called me up and said, "Mrs. Corwin said her son saw you in a movie.")

There were quite a few things I appreciated while we were making the record: for instance the energy of Dave Getz's driving tom-toms in "Combination Of The Two" and the abrupt shifting of gears into different key centers in that same song.

When we got to overdubbing the background vocals on "I Need A Man To Love", the choice to make the album in a studio paid off. Those same vocal parts *("No, it just can't be")* on the band's audition tapes, captured on the "Janis Joplin Live at Winterland" album (see the next Chapter/Track), were really ragged. So now we made them more powerful by doubling them, as the horns had been doubled on the Blood, Sweat & Tears album earlier.

The first sessions were done in NYC and then we took a little break.

> And Albert, with some urgency, wanted me to produce another of his artists, The Electric Flag. The Flag was in transition: Mike Bloomfield, the stellar guitar player who co-founded the group, was gone, along with a couple of other key players, leaving drummer Buddy Miles and bassist Harvey Brooks in charge. The horn section seemed to have sprung from the Omaha connections of their excellent organist, Herbie Rich.

The Flag sessions were to happen in Columbia's Studios in LA on Hollywood Boulevard. And, since I would be there and Big Brother was based less than 400 miles away in San Francisco, it was decided that their sessions would resume there too.

So I was a busy beaver, recording two albums at once: the Electric Flag in the afternoon and, across the hall at night, Big Brother and Janis.

> Since the pianist for The Flag had left the band, I happily slipped onto the piano bench.

Late in the afternoon one day, Janis came storming into the Electric Flag session surrounded by her huge aura, saw me playing the piano and said, "Hey, You!"

> (That was what she called me.)

"Hey, You! How come you're playing piano on <u>their</u> record and not on mine, Mother Fucker?"

(That was another of her affectionate names for me.)

So that night, for her recording session, she insisted I play piano on her song, "Turtle Blues". I plopped myself down in front of the piano and gave it my best shot. But this was before I had played the blues much and I was lousy.

And that recording lives on – which, to me, is unfortunate. (I've gotten a lot better playing the blues since then.)

> Someone decided we should add the sound of a glass breaking at the end of Peter's guitar solo on "Turtle Blues" to suggest the ambiance of a bar.
> That was fine with me because it was audio slapstick and I've always been a fan of slapstick.

"Cheap Thrills" was the kickoff for Janis's Big-Time career. After it was released, her vocals on "Piece Of My Heart" and "Summertime" were heard around the world.

And her sudden, enormous popularity put her on dangerous ground.

> Just imagine. In San Francisco she had been able to walk through Golden Gate Park and be warmly greeted with smiles from her Flower Power "family". But, once she was on the covers of magazines, she couldn't step out the door of her hotel without encountering a crush of fans.

And in that respect she became a tragic soul – thrown into the world's spotlight faster and harder than she'd ever imagined. But Albert Grossman was her rock. Her shield from the outside world.

They clearly loved each other and also depended on each other: Janis on Albert for protection, Albert on Janis for money.

> There's a line in the movie, "Inside Llewyn Davis" where the main character plays his heart out on a soulful ballad auditioning for Albert. And F. Murray Abraham, as Albert, says, "Frankly, I don't see any money in it."

Pretty accurate, I think.

Albert saw a lot of money in Janis even while he was fascinated by her and doted on her at the same time.
A few years later, whenever she was in Woodstock, Janis always had a home base at Albert's house on Striebel Road. I'd see her psychedelic Porsche convertible parked in the driveway.

She seemed more relaxed there than anywhere else.

She had a stellar career. Her popularity knew no bounds.

It became too much for her.

> Did she die in bed? In the bathroom? On the floor? Or was that
> Elvis? Or Jimi? Jim Morrison? Sid Vicious? Kurt Cobain? Michael
> Jackson?

> Each of them wearied by the road, by fame, adulation, by more
> stardom than they could handle.
> Did we suck them up?
> Are we to blame?
> Or is it our human nature to try to suck as much out of our pop
> idols as we can, just as their celebrity comes with an obligation to
> try to satisfy our thirst?

When we had finished recording and got ready to mix, we still had to
satisfy the expectation for a <u>live</u> album. We had to create the illusion of a
large auditorium.

From the original Winterland test session tapes, we retained concert pro-
moter Bill Graham's intro ("Four gentlemen and a great, great broad")
and his closing benediction, ("Have a happy Sunday") followed by the
liturgical music he had chosen to close out the evening.
Other than that, "Ball and Chain" is the only performance on the album
that was actually from those live tapes. Well, it's 90% live because we
substituted a new guitar solo for the original.

And that eventually led to some more trouble.

TRACK 28 – "NOT EQUIPPED"

That guitar solo on "Ball and Chain" became Exhibit A in what might have been called an Evidentiary Hearing.

Some years later Sony, the inheritor of Columbia Records, issued an album titled "Janis Joplin Live at Winterland" that they maintained came from "recently discovered tapes". Producer Elliott Mazer, who had assisted me in the completion of "Cheap Thrills", called me up and said, "Hey, those are the test recordings you did, the audition tapes from Winterland in 1968. Are you getting royalties?"

I wasn't.

When I reached someone at Sony, they wouldn't believe that the tapes were actually part of the "Cheap Thrills" recording project I had done, maintaining that they were "discovered" in their vault, unlabeled, by Bob Irwin, a detective-type who specialized in combing the vaults. Whether or not any original labels had been destroyed, I put together an Evidence Tape. On the left channel was "Ball and Chain" from the "Janis Joplin Live at Winterland" album and on the right channel was the same song from "Cheap Thrills".

It was so obvious that they were identical, except for the replaced guitar solo. Even a Martian could hear it.

But when I played it for the suits who ran the most influential record company in the world, a company deaing in music, they said, "We are not equipped to make musical decisions."

I am going to repeat that because that sentence is so precious to me.

The lawyers and executives who ran Sony, the most powerful record company in the world, a company dealing in <u>music</u>, said, "<u>We are not equipped to make musical decisions</u>."

In general and completely, truer words were never spoken.
They said they'd have to refer it to their A&R department.

Meeting with Steve Berkowitz, a Sony A&R guy, I proved that I produced the "Janis Live At Winterland" recordings (and got a fabulous sushi lunch out of our meeting in the tower of the Sony building) but then came more trouble.

Having proven to Sony, through Steve Berkowitz, that I was the producer of "Janis Live At Winterland", they told me that they had assumed there was no producer for the "Janis Live At Winterland" recordings, based on Bob Irwin's claim that he had found the tapes in an unlabeled box.
So they had already divided up all the royalties between Janis's estate and Bob Irwin as the producer and there was nothing left for me.
If I was unhappy with that (which I was) they suggested I contact <u>Janis's estate.</u>

Are you still with me?

Peter Shukat, incidentally the younger brother of my one-time manager, Scott Shukat, acted as the attorney for Janis's estate. His hard-headed negotiating skills brought me to tears.

(Example:

Peter: "How can you be completely certain you were there for every single moment of the recording of every song at Winterland? You may have gone to the bathroom."

Me: "Are you <u>serious</u>?")

There are hundreds of lawyer jokes. Feel free to insert one of your own here.

TRACK 29 – MYRA

"**H**i, Myra."

I hadn't seen Myra Friedman for years, since we had both been working for Columbia Records, she as a publicist, me as a fledgling producer.

Now I bumped into her in Albert Grossman's office. We caught up.

She had had a lot of highlights in her life since then. One of the biggies was that Bernard Goetz, the Subway Gunman, lived in her apartment building and had asked her to hide his gun.

Another (and this is what brought her to Albert's office) was that she had written a good biography of Janis.
She made a comment about my leaving my name off of Janis's "Cheap Thrills" album because I didn't like it and didn't want to be associated with it.

(Truth, Lies, Hearsay?)

I said, "But Myra, that's not true! That's not why I left my name off." And I explained to her that Howard Alk, while we were working together on "You Are What You Eat", had, at the time, convinced me that "credit corrupts".

That is to say, if you put your name on a project, a part of you is thinking, "How will my work on this project affect my reputation?" And you'll make compromises that will corrupt the purity and honesty of your work.

But, if you leave your name off and work anonymously, you won't be worried about your reputation and you'll be free to take chances—"make great art"—even if it goes beyond the bounds of what people may want or like.

That notion sounded like common sense to me and a noble, lofty thing to do. Ars Gratia Artis. Art For Art's Sake.

So I decided I'd leave my name off the next album I signed on to do, which was to be "Cheap Thrills".

Myra listened politely, paused, then said, "Well, that's not the truth. You left your name off because you hated the record."

Well, that wasn't the truth—at least as I recalled it.

Then recently Dave Getz, the drummer in Big Brother, reminded me that I was less than delighted with the experience of making "Cheap Thrills". So, coupling that fact with Howard's notion, it would have made twice as much sense to me then to leave my name off the album cover – even though I'd always enjoyed seeing it on that 12-inch cardboard square.

So, though my memory of "credit corrupts" might suggest a deeper, more interesting philosophy, Myra's guess turns out to be valid too.

And I can understand that her version, in its simplicity and logic, is easier to believe.

Both things were probably true.

Interesting.

TRACK 30 – THE FLAG, CASS AND ASSORTED HOLLYWOOD GLITTERATI

N ame-dropping makes me uncomfortable but, in the case of Hollywood, it's inevitable.

The hang-out buddies of the people I was working with looked just like people I'd seen on the silver screen. But they weren't look-alikes. They were actually them.

So I shot pool with actor Peter Lawford (JFK's brother-in-law and member of Sinatra's "rat pack"), shared a joint with Brandon DeWilde (the little kid in "Shane"), and met teen star Shaun Cassidy (which was a big deal to my kids at the time). But a bigger deal for me was joking with comedian Tommy Smothers (the wilder of The Smothers Brothers whose groundbreaking TV show was cancelled by CBS because of its anti-Vietnam war position)

Up till my sessions recording The Electric Flag and Big Brother in day/ night tandem, my exposure to Hollywood had been limited to the inside of a studio and an occasional meal outside.

But then I joined The Flag for a couple of LA gigs they had booked. The first was at the Whiskey a Go Go. That night is permanently impressed in my memory because the volume of Harvey Brooks's Marshall amp was permanently impressed on my eardrums that night.

The Whiskey was smoky and crowded that night. The stage wasn't very large so my Wurlitzer electric piano had been set up directly in front of Harvey's amp. I remember Buddy Miles counting off the first number. I remember my hands heading down toward the keys for the first chord of the number. But I don't think they ever made it.

Because a microsecond earlier Harvey's big bass note came booming out of his amp behind my head which re-shaped my normally round skull into a ping-pong paddle.

I had never heard anything so loud and don't wish to ever again.

But it was the second of those LA gigs that opened many new doors.

It was in a larger club with a stage that, thank heaven, left plenty of room for me to get away from Harvey's amp. I think the club was called The Kaleidoscope.

We played our set and things were going great until the owner of the club dropped the show curtain at exactly midnight in the middle of a song, which he had warned us he was going to do.

Bummer.

But in the audience that night was John Sebastian, later to become my friend and co-resident in Woodstock. At that time however Sebastian was living in a tipi on a piece of property on Barham Boulevard lovingly known as "The Farm".

Sensing our crestfallen-ness, he invited us to a party that was going on there and Harvey and I took him up on his invitation.

What a party!

I had seen semi-structured debauchery like this in the movies but I'd never seen it in real life. It wasn't an orgy or a riot or anything out of control. It was just plain fun with no restrictions. People were laughing, improvising games, making music, carrying on with an unbridled joy that could only be the result of conviviality, talent and psychedelics.

Cyrus Faryar and Renais were the residents, along with Fred and Lynn Williams in the garage, Sebastian in his tipi, Annie Thomas, who was instrumental in introducing tie-dying to America, and some more terrific people.

The atmosphere was as permeated with hippiedom as Haight-Ashbury but not as funky. Sebastian and I each hooked up with our second wives there. (His marriage to Catherine took. Mine with Brooke didn't.) I eventually produced an album for Cyrus there in his living room with legendary rockabilly guitarist, James Burton, the drummer from "Bread", Mike Botts, Brian Garafalo on bass and other stellars.

> Cyrus's album, "Islands", had some wonderful surprises: Dick Rosmini singing an ancient sea chanty, songs by Harry Nillson and Fred Neil, and of course Cyrus, a member of the Modern Folk Quartet, with his suede baritone voice and a bevy of stringed instruments.

I was staying at the Château Marmont Hotel, living out of a suitcase and liberally handing out Big Pink albums. The gratitude that the locals felt for that album resulted in invitations to all kinds of parties where I met music celebs like Stephen Stills, Keith Moon from The Who, David Crosby and Mama Cass Elliot.

Actually I met Cass at a Frank Zappa concert. She was just separating from The Mamas and the Papas, loved the Big Pink album and asked if I would produce her first solo album.

> The Zappa concert was noteworthy in that it marked the first appearance of Eric Clapton in Hollywood. The buzz at the concert was that Clapton was going to show up and play. And he did. But every time he stepped to the front of the stage to take a solo,

Zappa, not to be outshone, snuck behind him and turned Eric's amp down.

Cass was a wonderful person, as warm as her voice, and a lot of fun to be with as well.

The album we did together was titled "Dream a Little Dream of Me", a follow-up of her hit produced by Lou Adler. The album tended toward the psychedelic so much that Cass told me later that Lou Adler was going to sue us. (To my knowledge he never did.)

We recorded songs by John Hartford, Graham Nash, Leonard Cohen and me. Plas Johnson, immortalized by playing the tenor sax theme for The Pink Panther, played on the record, as well as drummer Hal Blaine, James Burton and Harvey Brooks.

> Cass asked Harvey to be her musical director for her notorious Vegas debut. Things didn't turn out well for her in Vegas but I know no more than that, other than what I've read; it'll be up to Harvey to provide the details. Cass can't cuz, sadly, she's gone. But it was not a good memory for her, that's for sure. So I never asked her about it.

Some years later, after I had married C.C., the woman I earlier referred to as "my final and greatest wife", Cass visited us on her way to England. It was our great good fortune to see her again. I say "our" because it turned out that C.C and Cass knew each other from many years earlier and so we all enjoyed catching up.

> It was Memorial Day weekend, 1974. Some of our neighbors were celebrating with a barbecue and we brought Cass along.
> Duke Ellington had just died and I arranged "Mood Indigo" for some local kids who were just learning how to play their horns and Cass sang it. What a sweet thing it was to see those young beginners joining a real pro in a tribute to a true Master.

> We were lucky to have hung out with her again before she left for London for the last time.

* * *

While I was on the West Coast, Leon Russell asked if I would sub for him and play piano with Bonnie and Delaney for a concert at one of the ballrooms in San Francisco. Leon had another gig one night. So I was to play Friday night and Leon on Saturday.

> Friday went fine but when Leon came up to play the next night, I learned something new about gospel piano-playing.

> When I had played on that Friday night I would stop playing in between the songs. But on Saturday Leon would keep noodling in between the songs while Delaney rapped, in the manner of a gospel church service. That was the way it was supposed to be done.

After those gigs in San Francisco, I drove back down to LA with bass player, Carl Radle and a few days later that whole Bonnie and Delaney crew and a bunch of other Hollywood musicians showed up in a studio to celebrate Leon's birthday.

The subject of drugs will inevitably come up in these stories. To write about rock and roll and omit any mention of drugs would be like putting up a scarecrow without a pole.

The drug in question that night point was angel dust, the hot new drug-du-jour on the scene.

Angel dust was no light weight. No one was quite sure what it was. The phrase "animal tranquilizer" was in the air but that didn't seem to discourage the fearless drug explorers of the time.

Leon's birthday session started with all of us in a circle singing "Will the Circle Be Unbroken" and then it developed into a free-for-all with at least 20 musicians playing whatever they wanted at the same time. That same song went on without a break for the entire event, maybe 8 hours.

It was so loud that Bobby Keyes was playing his tenor for his girlfriend who was backed into a corner and whose head was only a few inches from the bell of Bobby's horn. Could she hear him? I can't say for certain.

At one point I fell asleep right on top of Dave Mason's amp while it was turned up to max.

I heard that Leon and some others went back into the studio some days later to hear what they had wrought.

I shudder at the thought.

TRACK 31 – OLDE WOODSTOCKE

Ah, the comforting arms of the mountains of New York State! I was glad to get back home.

When I moved back east after my California adventures I no longer had a pad in New York City so I settled in Woodstock.

Woodstock was a very cordial village. And all the people there who were associated with the music business seemed to be one big family. It was never necessary to call somebody up when you wanted to drop by. You just got in your car, drove up and knocked on their door.

(Because of that, the occasional romantic affairs in town were never a secret.
   "You can tell by the car
   where the liaisons are.")

In many respects it was like a typical, picket fence, small New England town. You knew the cops, the post office lady, the grocer, the guy who fixed your plumbing.
There were parades on holidays, Santa Claus showed up on the village green before Christmas. There were softball games every weekend. Albert and Paul Butterfield, who were fiercely proud of their Chicago roots, introduced the "Chicago softball" which was a bigger and softer model and which we tried for one week before booing it off the ball field.

Because it was a music town there were jam sessions, planned and impromptu. Many of them were held at the house of Jim Rooney, a wonderful guy, once part of a duo with banjoist Bill Keith.
His wife had the melodious name of Sheila Mooney Rooney.

> I didn't have very many sessions at my house but I do recall one in particular. I had found this special little piano that had independent pickups behind each string and Bob Dylan came over to my basement to check it out.

But Bob's notoriety notwithstanding, the most noteworthy event in my basement as far as I'm concerned was The Pool Table Grudge Match.
Paul Butterfield's Chicago-pride extended to his expertise at pool, which he absorbed in Second City bars. Geoff and Maria Muldaur also lived in town and Geoff had eventually heard enough of Paul's braggadocio and challenged him to a match on a pool table that, through diverse circumstances, ended up in my basement.

> At the time, cocaine had come into prominence as the socially acceptable drug-of-choice (though not with me). The two combatants each seemed to have decided that cocaine would ensure his chance of victory so they had brought an entire pill bottle of white powder that sat on the edge of the pool table next to the cube of chalk as they began their match at around dinnertime.

I watched for a while then left and came back several times that night before going to bed.

When I woke up in the morning they were still at it, the pill bottle was empty and Butter was several hundred dollars in the hole. In an attempt to catch up he was challenging Geoff to double-or-nothing but his situation wasn't improving. Finally Geoff, who had honed his skills in high-class private clubs and residences, told Butter that he could beat him left-handed—which he then did. The next day Paul asked Albert to pay his debt for him.

(I imagine Albert complied, with terms that were beneficial to the lender.)

ABG.
Albert Grossman. He used to initial things with those initials. ABG.

Not that he initialed many things. Or signed many things. Except when it was to his advantage.

He and I never had a paper contract between us. When I found myself short of money, he'd give me a check. Enough to pay my bills.

> His negotiating skills reached beyond the music business. Robbie Robertson told me a story about something that occurred when Bob Dylan was touring in Australia.
> Australia had tough anti-drug laws at the time and someone had reported to the police that there was cannabis use going on in Bob's hotel room.
> There was a knock at the door and the narco-cops, very anti-Dylan, came in intent on searching the room. Albert smooth-talked and assisted them during their search, all the while hiding a significant block of hash under the hat on his head.

Albert was a hands-on manager. He had a very keen business sense and wasn't shy about telling artists what he thought they should do.

> I've heard it said that I insisted Janis get a different band after "Cheap Thrills". Albert very well may have asked my opinion about it. I don't recall him doing so. But, in any event, it wasn't my place to make any decision like that, much less to insist. It was none of my business. Albert and Janis had the power.

Albert's house was the hangout-of-choice. A beautiful, classic old farmhouse, it was sort of a salon. Showbiz celebrities passing through stopped to pay their respects and to enjoy Albert's generous hospitality and that of his wife, Sally. There was a cozy, stone den where laughter and smoke filled the air. There was always excellent food usually prepared by Yvette, his French cook. There was a separate studio with a sauna and an excellent sound system. The place was full of interesting antiques and artifacts and there were bedrooms enough for all.

Albert & Sally. Note position of cigarette: an Albert "thing".

Albert was acquiring property. He got it into his head to build a recording studio. He asked me for advice and of course I recommended Columbia's old Studio A.

I gave him the measurements but he made a mistake: thinking that bigger was better, he doubled everything which resulted in a cavern too big for anything to sound good.

Fortunately he had added a smaller room which became the room everyone used at Bearsville Studios.

I worked on albums for Bobby Charles, Jackie Lomax, Seals and Crofts and other artists there.

Years after it opened, staff engineer John Holbrook redesigned the big room to favorable effect. Its quirky acoustics lent character to later recordings by R.E.M., Dave Matthews, and others.

When it came to the building of the studio office complex, he hired a crusty, skilled local craftsman named Paul Cypert. Earlier Paul had built my house out of an old barn, including a wooden circular staircase built from scratch that Albert admired. Paul duplicated that staircase for Albert's recording studio and ended up building the Bearsville Theater, two restaurants and a TV studio for Albert as well, along with any other project that came along.

The two were approximately the same age and though Albert had all the experience of a world traveler and Paul had hardly traveled more than 50 miles from home, they recognized a soul connection in each other. They were both fun-loving nonconformists and they remained very close pals until Albert's death.

After Albert's memorial service in Woodstock, I went over to the Bearsville complex and I saw Paul on his bulldozer smoothing the earth down over Albert's grave.

TRACK 32 – FESTIVAL

I n 1969 Michael Lang, who had previously promoted a small-by-comparison rock festival in Miami, got financial backing from John Roberts and Joel Rosenman (who – get this coincidence—was a class-mate of mine at Princeton!). And they came up with the idea of a music festival in Woodstock.

But the town board, sensing that the enormity of the project would burst the town at the seams, rescinded their original permit and refused to allow it to happen in Woodstock so Michael eventually located a dairy farm in Bethel to the southwest (actually in the Catskills' Borscht Belt) to stage the event and the festival still retained the name, "Woodstock".

Everyone's got a Woodstock Festival story and here's mine.
I knew the Festival was about to happen. Everybody did. We fol-lowed the saga from its inception as Michael's idea, through the Woodstock town board turning it down because of the antici-pated crowds and the final securing of the site owned by a farmer named Max Yasgur.

I knew half the people who were going to play and that, coupled with the fact that I hardly like to go out to hear music anyway, contributed to my lack of interest in the festival.

But as I listened to the news that weekend it seemed like it was a cultural event not to be missed. Yasgur's farm was actually closer to my house at that point than was downtown Woodstock so it seemed an easy matter to go check it out.

My second wife, Brooke and I had our morning orange juice and got in the car to drive over there. But when we got within a few miles there was a roadblock and, after I snowed the state cops with a bunch of famous names, they directed me to this heliport where we could catch a whirly bird into the festival itself.

The heliport was brand-new. Bulldozers had simply flattened the top of a hill so that a single helicopter could ferry people from there into the festival.

The helicopter had four passenger seats and we were given tickets for seats one and two. Another couple came along after us and got their tickets for seats three and four. We all climbed aboard and the rotors spun as we are about to lift off.

Suddenly a Red Cross van came wheeling up to the helicopter telling the pilot to wait because the chopper had to take "emergency medical supplies" to the site. That's another phrase chiseled into my memory. In the meantime I had been looking to the West from this hilltop and saw huge, billowing black thunderheads in the sky where I knew our weather came from.

Putting two and two together, it seemed that being dropped into this imminent weather catastrophe along with emergency medical supplies was not the greatest idea known to humanity. So we gave up our seats to the couple with seats three and four and decided to go home.

Coincidentally, because of the Sunday storm that soaked the Festival, we lost our electric power for almost a week.

That's my Woodstock Festival story.

Three days of freewheeling music and mud in Bethel, and voilà: a legend. And, within a week after that, the <u>influx</u> into the REAL Woodstock began.

Three times a day the Adirondack Trailways bus door would open at the real Woodstock's village green and disgorge more penniless, wannabe Bob Dylans.

He blows into town, guitar in hand
Lookin' like the hottest picker in the land.
Mr. Natural. Mr. Cool.
Gonna make some other pickers look the fool.

Takes his guitar out of the patched up sack
When the people heard him play, they made him put it back.

(Chos.) He stinked. He stinked.
Boy, did he stink.

(The Guitar Player – 1969)

TRACK 33 – SAMMY'S POOL HOUSE

s it happened, I seldom did a follow-up album with an artist after we had a hit album together.

Why? I don't know. Maybe they felt that they could do it on their own. Maybe somebody told them a different, hot, new producer would be perfect for them. Maybe I pissed them off.

(I actually HAVE pissed off at least one artist. She, who shall remain un-named for now, let the air out of my tires. I respect her for that unique way of expressing her frustration with me.

No, it wasn't Janis.)

But I did produce The Band's second album.

"Music From Big Pink" had all turned out well, we had become friends staying in pretty close contact since Big Pink was released and now I was based in Woodstock. So moving ahead together with the second album was a natural thing.

As we talked, it became clear that Robbie was having the same problem that most artists have after making their first record: new material. He and the others had lots of songs stockpiled for their debut album—the cream of the crop—but here came the prospect of a follow-up album and the straightest arrows from their quivers had already been shot.

Robbie and Dominique had just had their first child, Alexandra. Brooke, and I were her godparents. (Sort of by default. I remember Robbie saying,

"I guess you guys are her godparents." Not exactly a deep, heartfelt choice. But anyway…)

Robbie decided to take his family to Hawaii so that he would have some solitude to come up with new material.

Robbie's mother, "Mama Kosh" (rhymes with "gauche", though she was hardly gauche) was sort of a den mother to The Band. She would go along to help with the baby, and Brooke and I were invited too—I suppose I was there to help with Robbie's new songs.

> (We all rented a house with a view of the Pacific in Haewaolaaoui or someplace like that. The Hawaiian language has a surplus of vowels. They should maybe work out a trade agreement with Polish which has plenty of consonants to spare and could use some vowels.)

As it turned out, I didn't help Robbie with his new songs in Hawaii other than to listen to them as they were coming together and comment. But Robbie did help me with a new song of mine, "Davy's On The Road Again", a self-searching lyric in which I explained to myself why I made the break from my life five years earlier and ended up in Hawaii working on a rock 'n roll record.

I had completed the song but Robbie suggested adding a chorus and, right off the top of his head, he sang:

> *"Shut the door. Cut the light*
> *Davy won't be home tonight."*

I added:

> *"You can wait till the dawn rules in.*
> *You won't see your Davy again."*

and, voilà, a chorus.

I recorded the song on my own first album and Manfred Mann, after his success with "My Name Is Jack", recorded "Davy…" soon after.

Our vacation in Hula-land eventually ended and we met the other guys in The Band in Hollywood to record our second album.

Transportation:

We'd need cars. One of the folks who would frequent social gatherings at "The Farm" on Barham Boulevard was Jack Poet. His name sounds like a show biz nom de guerre but he actually owned a car dealership, Jack Poet Volkswagen. When he offered to supply us with free vehicles it seemed like a good deal. That is, until we saw the cars he had in mind. Jack was not your typical car dealer. He had an idea to get hippie artists to paint his VW Beetles with wild designs. It was The Sixties and he thought the painted VWs would become a trend and he would have the jump on all the other car dealers in LA, the US and, eventually, the world. He was, as you might imagine, wrong. But he had offered free vehicles to us and for a while we drove VW beetles around LA that were painted with daisies, ladybugs, chipmunks and various psychedelic designs.
But that "while" didn't last very long.

Now bear in mind that this was in 1969, waaaaaay back before cell phones, back before the internet. In fact, credit cards were a new thing.

I happened to have a credit card from the time I worked at Columbia Records. No one else at Sammy's house had one. So, when the desire arose among us for vehicles that didn't look like Disney billboards, I was sent to the Hollywood Hertz rent-a-car office along with Richard so that we could drive 2 cars back to the house.

I presented my card to the Hertz guy who got on the phone (remember: no computers), He spoke to someone at Hertz Central, answered "yes" to several questions that only he could hear, then reached into a drawer, pulled out a pair of scissors and said "It is duly cut in half."

(That's another weighty phrase etched in my memory.) Credit cards were so new I didn't realize they expired!

So, with 2 halves of a credit card, we called Albert who bailed us out, figuratively speaking.

Accomodations:

Through Albert's office, we were installed in a large house in the Hollywood Hills that had most recently been the property of the fabulous, multitalented entertainer, Sammy Davis Jr. during the period when he was married to photogenic Scandinavian actress, May Britt.

The five-and-and-one sixteenth of us who had been in Hawaii flew directly to LA. Rick and Richard had each married and their wives, Gracie and Jane respectively, came along for the ride. Garth and Levon were the only bachelors in the entourage.

One of the reasons for choosing Sammy's place was the pool house. That was to be where we would record.

Capitol Records had agreed to set us up with our own recording equipment, independent of their Hollywood and Vine facilities. There would be amps, a mixing board, an 8-track recording machine, speakers and even a clunky, old, but wonderful, EMT reverb plate. They would send a maintenance engineer out every couple of days to make sure the equipment was in great shape. But, other than that, there would be no recording engineer. We were on our own.

By this point I realized that I preferred to be in the room with the musicians rather than behind a glass in the control room. Being behind that control room glass made communication quite difficult: when I would hold down the talkback button to speak to the musicians on the other side of the glass, their microphones would be muted. So, though I might see their lips move in response, I couldn't hear anything they were saying until I finished talking and released the talkback button. Yuk!

Also I loved being there in the room where the music was actually happening instead of being physically removed from it.

It was a new thing to throw out the idea of a control room and set up the mixing console in the midst of the music but that's what we did.

It was a capacious room, one you can see in the photos that Elliott Landy shot for that album's jacket. If you look at the longshot photo with the mixing board in the console and my feet on it, you can imagine two rooms behind you. Down a short staircase was a bathroom that we sometimes used for additional echo and up a short staircase was Levon's bedroom, which also became a hangout area for listening and playing checkers.

Speaking of checkers, Rick and Levon were the most accomplished checker players. I was the worst. But Richard invented a new checker game called "Gimmees", the object of which was to <u>lose</u>. And he was the champ at that.

Beside being a different drummer, Richard marched to the beat of one. When all the guys grew beards, he grew a "neck beard". His clean-shaven face was surrounded by a thick wreath of hair and it looked like his face was peering out of a dried-up Christmas wreath.

We put packing blankets up on the walls to lessen the echo in the room and went shopping for instruments.

Levon found a vintage set of wooden drums in a pawn shop. We had heard a particular "moaning" tom-tom sound that Ringo got on the Beatles records and we worked to duplicate it. We ended up loosening the drum head except for one pair of lugs opposite each other that we tightened up.

> I'm told that, on YouTube, Ringo talks about trying to duplicate Levon's sound. Did he know he was actually trying to duplicate himself?

Garth and Richard chose a big upright piano with a nice full sound and easy action and we were off and running.

When we got the speakers installed we were anxious to try them out. It happened to be real late, maybe 3 AM. We were all big fans of Dr. John so we put on his new album and turned it up loud.

After 15 or 20 minutes, Dominique came running down to the studio shouting, "Robbie, zee cops, zee cops!" (She had a lovely French-Canadian accent.)

It seems that Sammy Davis Jr. had installed speakers outside by the pool and, in the wee small hours of the morning, Hollywood moguls and lackeys alike had been jolted out of their sleep by Dr. John's ramshackle chorus singing:

"My country, 'tis of thee
Sweet land of liberty

Of thee I sing."

("Patriotic Flag-waver", Mac Rebennack,1969)

I couldn't wait to get into the studio and start work. The prospect was delicious. But Capitol was a month late in getting the recording equipment together for us and we had allotted just 2 months in Sammy's house to record the album. This delay would have repercussions later.

We all knew we had the ability to make a record without any outside help.

I knew just enough about the engineering side of recording so that we wouldn't need the help (or intrusion) of an engineer.

Robbie told me pointedly that, in the process of making this record, his goal was to learn everything I knew about recording (which I told him in 5 minutes).
So he spent a lot of time himself at the recording console, experimenting and learning.

For instance, there's a photo of me playing the guitar in the inner sleeve of The Band's second album. I don't play guitar. In the photo you can see Robbie wearing headphones sitting at the board. I'm just the dummy guitarist playing away so that he can experiment with the sound.

(You wouldn't want to hear what I was playing.)

It would be an understatement to say that making this album was a lot of fun. As with the first album I was happy to be a contributor to the music beyond the producer's usual role of just saying, "Okay, we're rolling. Take one." And now, with no control room glass to frustrate conversation, we were all just in one big room making music.

It was "the lab" again, working patiently on each song to try to get the best out of it. But this time we had more control.

During the month's delay while waiting for the recording equipment to arrive, we worked on the material.

Finally Capitol delivered the recording equipment.

With only one month to record material when we had hoped for two, the guys asked me if I knew a doctor who could help get us some pills "to make us more efficient".

This was all new to me. I had never taken anything like speed before except No-Doz, an over-the-counter caffeine pill, to help me finish a paper in college. But a good friend of mine, Phil Weinstein, who appeared in this narrative earlier when he had been a drummer at Princeton, had become a brain surgeon and lived in San Francisco. Phil, though not in the habit of recommending pills willy-nilly, was sympathetic and helped us out by sending us a prescription for what Rick referred to as "overweight high school girls' diet pills".

They worked but, for the first time, I felt a craving for cigarettes— which, thank God, disappeared when the diet pills disappeared.

We had bought a second piano and put it in another room in the house. And though Robbie didn't ordinarily play piano, he wrote "The Night They Drove Old Dixie Down" on that piano. He had enough technique to kick the arrangement off with that ascending left hand bass line.
We settled into the studio and decided to record "Dixie" first.

Once in front of the microphones, we were able to tinker with the sound of the instruments, try different microphones, etc.

Since it was the first song we recorded, we moved slowly and carefully. After that, it would generally take us about two days to record a song. On the first day, we'd practice it, repeating it over and over and over again to get comfortable with it and then knock off for the night. The next day we'd come back and pick up where we left off until we eventually got a take.

As we were recording "Dixie" I realized that it was sort of setting the tone for one of the themes that was to run through these recording sessions: the common man, the working folks, rurality (if that's a word).

Garth had by now put together quite a complicated rig of instruments and effects for these recordings. For "Dixie" he got a harmonica sound out of a clavinet with a wah-wah pedal and then, for effect, overdubbed an actual, bona fide trumpet over the fade at the end.

Though we tried to do as much live recording as possible, we <u>did</u> do more overdubbing on this album than on "Big Pink" which was mostly recorded on 4 tracks. This time we had the opportunity to use all the tracks on an 8 track recording machine and we took advantage of the opportunity.

> Years later, Robbie was in NYC for a promotional tour of something-or-other and he asked me to meet him at a TV studio where he was booked on a morning TV show. He decided to do "… Dixie …" and assembled quite a crew of musicians to help out. Imagine my surprise when Robbie asked me to sing the very very very very high harmony part that Richard sang on the original record.
> I fell far short and almost ruptured several parts of my anatomy trying to squeeze out those high notes in tune.

When we started working on "Cripple Creek" Garth had the idea of getting his clavinet to sound like a Jew's harp.

> It's sometimes called a "juice harp" in what I think is an over-zealous attempt to be politically correct. But it's an ancient folk instrument found in cultures all around the world – and that includes Appalachia and the rest of rural 19th century America.
> So Garth's thinking was right on.

We recorded "When You Awake" with its Appalachian Metaphysics. The innocence in Rick's voice was perfect for the character seeking the wisdom of "Ole", a wise old mountain sage.

> Around that time, pop culture was brimming with questions about The Meaning Of Life. It would be presumptuous of Robbie to answer that question in the lyric. So the answer from Ole that

the guys sang in the chorus was cryptic. For instance, his pre-diction, "You will be hangin' on a string from your ..." was left unfinished.

Then there was "Rockin' Chair", a touching portrait in the same vein. But, while the words of "When You Awake" suited the lightness of Rick's voice, Robbie wrote a beautiful, wistful lyric for this song and Richard's singing could touch your heart.
Here's Robbie, barely 30, writing about being 73.

> *"The Flying Dutchman's on the reef.*
> *It's my belief*
> *This hill's too steep to climb*
> *And the days that remain aren't worth a dime."*

Prophetic.

Listening to the 3 singers stack up for the choruses, I was struck by how great they sounded together.
It wasn't a blend like you'd get from, say, a family where all the vibratos and tone qualities genetically match. They were separate singers, each with a particular vocal quality.
As a result I could pick out the individual parts very clearly, Levon on the bottom, Rick in the middle and Richard singing falsetto on top.

It was a very interesting sound.

> The guys in the band were so inherently musical that they found picking up a new instrument and making music on it natural, challenging and fun.
> Levon was always open to suggestions and to learning something new, always humble, never haughty.
> We imagined a mandolin part for "Rockin' Chair" but there were more chords required than 99% of mandolin players would ever be asked to play.

So he and I sat down in facing chairs to figure it out. It remains one of my favorite memories of working with Levon. We each knew something the other didn't know. I heard some chords that he didn't know. He could play the mandolin better than I could. So together we figured out unconventional mandolin hand positions for chords that would fit the song.

Now we were on a roll again. We recorded a bunch of songs that never saw the light of day. Stuff they'd fooled around with in the basement of Big Pink: "Tell 'Em Tiny Montgomery Says Hello", "Yo, Heavy and a Bottle of Bread", "Orange Juice Blues" and "Look Out, Cleveland" which actually did make it onto the final album.

Robbie knew that Phil Spector had recorded a bunch of his hits at Gold Star Studios, so one day we left Sammy's house and went there to record and check out the famous Spector echo.
It turned out to be nothing more than a very live concrete space, much like the elevator shaft that Roy Hallee had used for Simon & Garfunkel's snare drum sound.

Back at Sammy's we started on "Across the Great Divide". For the intro, we started off, not in rhythm, but out of tempo ("rubato" in music lingo). Richard standing by the window in pain.
Six measures later the rhythm kicked in and we were off and running.

After we'd cut the track, Garth and I overdubbed those Band horns again.

If you're a shoemaker, you notice everyone's shoes. As a horn player in high school, I can't help but think that the horn sound Garth and I came up with was a big part of the Band's identification. Other horn parts that I heard on other recordings were clean, well-executed. Ours were rough – lots of "personality".

On 'Big Pink" I played a baritone horn, which I knew well from high school. For this song, Garth produced a peck-horn for me to play – a smaller instrument. After awhile I could get a sound out of it but the fingering was different from what I was used to – like playing a mandolin if you only knew how to play a guitar.

(In Italy, peck-horns were in every street band, like the ones in the Sicilian scenes in "The Godfather". But when Bob Giardinelli imported a bunch of them for his famous NYC brass instrument store, they went over like rubber lightning-rods. He was practically giving them away.)

We had visitors at Sammy Davis Jr.'s house. A lot of them were fellow musicians. Some were old friends who were now living on the West Coast.
But one day Albert called to tell us that the Italian filmmaker, Michelangelo Antonioni wanted to pay us a visit. He had just finished shooting a new movie called "Zabriskie Point" and had heard about The Band. I think he was considering us for the score.

By now we had a few songs recorded so we could play some rough mixes for the famous movie director. He sat down on Levon's bed, the site of many a checker game, and listened to what we'd recorded so far. Not speaking any English, he showed no signs of comprehension at all until Richard Manuel's opening lines from "Across the Great Divide":

"Standing by your window in pain,
Pistol in your hand..."

"Ah! Pistole! Pistole", exclaimed Antonioni, making the universal gun gesture with his right hand.

I don't know who did the music for "Zabriskie Point" but it wasn't us.

Back to work, we started to put together an arrangement for "Rag, Mama, Rag". Robbie had written a light-hearted lyric that promised a lot of fun.

Levon wanted to play the mandolin and Rick came up with a fiddle part and everything was fine except...

> I said, "Hey, every song needs a bass part and now we haven't got one."
> The guys said to me, "Well, you play the tuba, right?"
> Wrong.
> Like I said, I had played that baritone horn in high school but that's a much smaller instrument. I had never played a tuba before. The horn challenge was even greater than the little peck horn on "Across The Great Divide."
> But that didn't stop us. We rented a tuba and I huffed and puffed into it. It took so much wind I got dizzy a couple of times and actually started to see stars.

Richard played the drums on "Rag, Mama, Rag". Talk about a unique drum style! I called it "galumphy", which is not in any way a derogatory description.

Without the ability to play a drum roll or any of the rudiments that beginning drummers learn, he was hearing the drums as melody instruments and it didn't matter one bit if the discerning listener could detect a certain struggle going on between Richard and his tubs.

> (Incidentally, and this is only barely on the topic, no one stateside would ever call a drummer's equipment a "drum kit" until the British Invasion. As in the conquest of empires, those Invaders also brought new language with them. The use of "drum kit" versus "drum set" is an easy way to tell the Johnny-Come-Latelys from The Old Guard.)

Setting up for "Rag, Mama, Rag".

We were paying a lot of attention to the drum patterns in every song we tackled. We were quite particular.

"Jawbone" was intentionally extremely tricky, rhythmically. Each verse was different. The first was out of rhythm entirely, the second was in a shuffle beat, the third was in waltz-time, and the last was in straight 4/4. In addition the section before each chorus was in waltz-time and the chorus itself alternated between 4-beat measures and measures of 6 beats.

Holy Moley!

> So, once again, I was a living music chart for Levon, leaning on one of the gobos in front of the drums and pointing at a particular drum or cymbal as we entered each new section of the song and it would be time to change the rhythm pattern.

"Jawbone" was a portrait of a thief, and the subject of the next song we did, "Unfaithful Servant", was also a wrong-doer, although the lyric was sympathetic to the desperado who fled the scene after some falling-out.

> I asked Robbie if he was inspired by Stan and Dottie, a butler and cook that Albert had brought over from England, who ran off (I'm not sure they left empty-handed either).

Robbie didn't seem as interested in playing guitar solos as he was in writing the songs and playing the guitar parts that underpinned them. But for "Unfaithful Servant" he sat down and overdubbed a beauty that started with tremolos worthy of a Neapolitan mandolin serenade and employed bends and harmonics, all in service to the delicate mood of the song. It was a pleasure just to sit and hear him work out the solo until he got one he liked.

I was having a lot of fun working on these songs. But, even though I got to blow some horns and was inextricably tied into all the aspects of the recording, I was eager to put my hands on a piano. I got my chance on "King Harvest", the last song we recorded in the pool house.

The intros to each of the verses were beautiful bucolic landscape sketches over almost no rhythm at all.

> "Corn in the fields.
> 'Listen to the rice as the wind blows 'cross the water.
> King Harvest has surely come"

(No bones about it: Robbie Robertson can write a real good lyric.)

Then the tempo kicked in and we got this sort of "puffy" electric piano sound that, along with the bass and drums, was to glue the rhythm pattern together. But, because of the syncopation of the pattern, I was having a little trouble wrangling the piano part. Then Levon gave me some straightforward advice, "Pat your foot". That succinct nugget was all it took.

Now recall if you will that Capitol was a month late setting up all of our recording equipment. So, even though we didn't quite have enough songs to fill an album, the guys were booked for a performance in San Francisco based on the success of Big Pink.

So we finished up what we could and headed up the coast.

TRACK 34 – HYPNOSIS IN FRISCO, LOBSTER IN MANHATTAN

Robbie, as has been related ofttimes elsewhere, got real sick the day before the San Francisco show.

Probably nerves.

This was the first time the band would appear as The Band – a dream suddenly becoming reality and maybe, just maybe, the pressure was too much for him.

Anyway, he couldn't walk, he couldn't talk, he got fevers, chills, warts, ingrown toenails, quinsy – whatever he could get. All kinds of specialists in the medical profession were called but none could find anything wrong with him. It looked like the Momentous Concert might have to be cancelled.

Robbie, Levon, me, Rick and Albert with a gesture that says, "So?"

Once again, my college buddy, Phil Weinstein, drummer and brain surgeon, came to the rescue.

He came to take a look but couldn't come up with a remedy. However he did make a suggestion: he thought it might be psychological and knew of a hypnotist whom he thought might be effective.

So we called him up: Dr. Pierre Clement.

Dr. Clement made the house call to the Seal Rock Inn Motel and went to work.

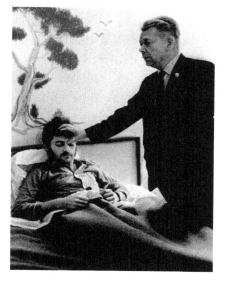

First he made a tree grow out of Robbie's head,
then he gave him some magic beans.

But whatever he did, it worked. Robbie went on stage the next night and, as he relates, above all the music and applause, all he heard were the magic words of Dr. Clement whispered from the wings.

The concert had been scheduled based on the popularity of "Music From Big Pink", their first album.

Halfway through the show someone in the audience actually yelled, "Now play side two!" (referring to that first album)—which was sort of an accurate comment given the fact that the guys didn't really know the material we had just been recording for the second album well enough to play it in public.

After the concert we went back to New York City to finish the album at Jerry Ragavoy's Hit Factory studio.

Working in a studio a few blocks north of Times Square was certainly a different vibe than we had at Sammy's house.

The change made us all a little giddy.
Instead of eating the cooked-with-love meals that our wives prepared in LA, we were ordering dinners delivered from any one of Manhattans' panoply of eateries. We soon hit on a favorite entree, Lobster Thermidor, a dish that takes a lot of work, one we'd never have at home. Rick called it "Lobster Thermomedor".

We picked up where we'd left off. We had rehearsed "Jemima Surrender" but hadn't gotten a good take of it before we had to pull up our tent stakes in California.

Richard played drums in a way that made the song bump along like a jalopy on 3 wheels that still managed to happily get to its destination and Garth played a rollicking piano part.
Then Garth and I overdubbed our "horn section" and Robbie added some guitar fills and a short solo

Jerry Ragavoy didn't trust us to be our own engineers with the Hit Factory's recording paraphernalia – and I don't blame him. Young Joe Zagarino would be our recording engineer

But one night suddenly all the equipment seemed to be breaking down.

We were on the verge of a fine take and, poof, some electronic nightmare occured.

So we stopped work, got a maintenance engineer on the case and tried again.

Then another breakdown. Start. Stop. Start. Stop. Start. Stop …

It was real frustrating.

By then it was well past 2 AM and we'd eaten as much Lobster Thermidor as was humanly possible so we decided to call it quits for the night.

> We hired a rock 'n roll limo to take us all and drop each one off wherever we were staying. On a street corner across Seventh Avenue from Sheridan Square we saw two guys arguing vigorously. They looked like bums. So let's call them that. Two bums yelling at each other on a street corner in the middle of the night. Arms and hands flying, jumping up and down.
>
> We asked the driver to change course a little so we could hear what in the world was going on. "What are they saying?"
>
> As we pulled up within earshot we heard one yell at the other, "It's a technical nation!"
>
> Richard would repeat that phrase each time we encountered a new glitch with the studio equipment.
>
> "It's a technical nation."

The last song we recorded was a beautiful ballad, "Whispering Pines". It was a melody that Richard had written but as yet he had no lyrics for it.

Robbie wrote the words and afterwards he told me he'd never written a song like that before. I suppose what he meant was a forlorn lyric about lost love. It was more like a lyric that Richard might have written.

Robbie also told me he'd never write a song in the first person, the inference being that it would be too personal. Of course, he did write songs in the first person but the narrator in those songs would be a character he invented, not Robbie himself.

So that was the last song we recorded.

Garth added some refinements to his earlier parts on some of the other songs, working late into the night which has become his preferred schedule.
I could never keep pace with his nocturnal time-table. I'm a diurnal creature. So I'd either fall asleep right there or say goodnight and go home.

We were done. We went back to Woodstock. The packaging was put together for the album. Elliott Landy supplemented the studio shots he took in LA with a couple of shots in Rick's Woodstock house.

The album was called "The Band" which, being the second album, is like calling your second child "Junior".

TRACK 35 — SIX CHARACTERS

I knew those guys real well. We spent a lot of time in the studio but we also just hung out.

Here are a few fragments of recollection that don't necessarily fit anywhere else.

Levon.

Levon was authentic "country". He was full of stories about growing up near the Delta and you can read a lot of them in his biography, "This Wheels' On Fire".

I remember one in particular that isn't in his book. He told me this one day when we were discussing religion. In his grade school in Arkansas, when the teacher read the roll for attendance each student had to respond with a Bible verse. When his name was called, he always answered, "Present. 'Jesus wept'". That happens to be the shortest verse in the Bible but, nonetheless, it qualifies. So, as Levon told it, except for a few goodie-goodies who reeled off extensive Biblical excerpts, everyone quoted that same short verse and the classroom was awash with Jesus's tears.

Rick.

Rick was from southern Ontario, Canada's "banana belt" (as warm as it gets in the Land To The North) – the farm country of Ontario. As a teen he had been training as a butcher's assistant but, understandably, his sights were on a less bloody arena – generally speaking. He led a variety of bands before being recruited by Ronnie Hawkins. He told me he would be his own "advance man" for his band's gigs, going to a town a week ahead of their performance and papering the telephone poles with flyers announcing their upcoming engagement.

Rick understood publicity. He once told me that if I wanted to be noticed I should shave my head and paint half of it purple. He was always coming up with ideas and suggestions, sometimes screwball, often useful. He was fun to hang out with.

Richard

One day while we were rehearsing for the first album and most of the guys were living in the Big Pink house, I noticed this huge scab on Richard's forearm, the size of a jumbo egg.

Here's what had happened. Being guys, with no home-making chops whatsoever, when the light bulbs in the bathroom gave out, they simply moved a table lamp into the bathroom and plugged it in next to the sink. Richard told me that he would wake from the previous night's revelry, go to the bathroom sink, lean on the lampshade and closely check out his condition in the mirror.

Well, one day a non-guy (that is, a woman guest) was in the house and woke up first. She went into the bathroom and removed the lampshade for a better look at herself in the mirror. Richard was the next one to wake and, checking himself out in the mirror, leaned on the bare light bulb until he smelled something burning. Himself.

Garth

Whereas I would be the first to criticize myself for being flip and blurting things out without thinking, Garth is the opposite. Ask him a simple question and you're likely to hear him pause long enough to reflect and frame an accurate answer which may last for a few minutes – or days.

One night C.C. and I had him over for dinner. As we sat down at the table, I told him that I'd just done some sessions with drummer Jerry Marotta who would play a Gameboy device between takes.

Then as the leisurely meal progressed, Garth began a slow narrative which eventually led to LA, musicians he played with including The Flying Burrito Brothers. By the time we were having dessert, he got around to Sneaky Pete who played steel guitar with that band. His tale of Pete went on slowly until, just as we were finishing, he said, "Sneaky Pete played a Game Boy too."

Garth has long rhythms.

They were sometimes a single organism: Rick, the heart, Richard, the soul, Levon, the guts, Garth, the intellect ... but I struggle with this metaphor when it comes to Robbie.

Robbie

With his double-barreled contribution as both the principal writer and imaginative guitarist, I might say he was cumulatively the biggest contributor to The Band.

At the same time, Robbie thought big and spoke hopefully about plans beyond The Band. He was a movie fan and wondered if some day he might be able to work with film-makers he admired, like Ingmar Bergman.

Eventually it was Robbie who broke up The Band when he felt uncomfortable within its confines for a variety of reasons. Sort of like John Lennon's self-removal from The Beatles.

He was both very much in The Band and, in his objectivity and detachment, separate from it.

Me

There's no denying that part of me longed to be a part of The Band—the part that ignored the trials of life as a musician-on-the-road. I had already asked Robbie if I could join up and had been rebuffed.

Also there's another fact concerning me and The Band which you may find surprising: I'm a musician. I'm a writer. I've got no head

for business. Economics was the only course I flunked in college.
So. ......

Newsflash: I receive no royalties for producing "Music From Big Pink" nor the second album, "The Band".

That's true.

How'd that happen?

Originally the guys in The Band were signed to Albert Grossman and we all received our royalties through him. We each got equal shares. However, a few years later, they changed things so the guys would get their royalties directly from Capitol Records.
I had no business manager watching out for me at the time and I certainly wasn't watching out for myself, so I fell through the cracks. There was no arrangement for Capitol to pay me.

It'd be nice if that situation were straightened out now and the others or their heirs would fork over 1/6 of their future checks to me. But there's about as much chance of that happening as water-skiing on the Sahara. And that ain't gonna happen.

Unfortunately.

INTERMISSION—TURN THE RECORD OVER

A t this point My-Life-In-Rock-And-Roll had reached a sort of pinnacle.

With the completion of The Band's second album, things slowed down for me. And I really appreciated that. C.C. and I had recently wed and, with two pre-school kids, I was ready to head down the gentle slope from Rock and Roll FRENZY toward the peaceful EQUANIMITY of maturity.

But it's not as if my life ended then and there. There were quite a few surprises that would show up on the paths that The Fates laid out for me:

Unexpected projects.
Memorable people.
More stories.

And some of those events have stuck in my memory because of those stories.

So I'm going to string some of them together, although I may depart a little from the chronological order I've been trying to maintain in this memoir so far.

And, as I was comfortably settling into a more mellow life in the early 70's, I invite you to comfortably settle into reading on.

TRACK 36 — THE TALE OF THREE ACCOUNTANTS

This isn't Hearsay. It's true. It could read like one of those Dickens stories where pitiful misfortunes pile up and where drool drips from the lips of unsavory characters as they rub their hands together in anticipation of fleecing Our Hero. In this tale Our Hero happened to be me.

Back in 1972, after The Band's initial success, Albert had decided we all needed accountants to handle our business. So he'd brought 2 of them to Sammy Davis Jr's house for us to meet. All the other guys chose David Braun, a smooth Hollywood bean-counter whose clients were a list of Who's-Whos. I chose the other guy, Sy Rosen from NYC.
Braun was super-slick. Sy was a mensch.

Things were fine for years. I went on my merry way all year and, as each April came around, Sy would tell me to write a check to the IRS.

Then, as The Fates laid it out for me, having left Rock and Roll Frenzy by the end of the Seventies, I had moved into a different phase of work which from a pop record perspective might be seen as "The Lost Years".

I wasn't getting the calls to produce because I hadn't had a hit for years.

Which was OK with me because the most popular pop music then had become heavy metal and then disco. Both of which left me cold.

In the meantime, I wasn't producing so, in order to keep things afloat one winter, I took a job playing cocktail piano at The Oritami restaurant in Hackensack, New Jersey.

I would put on my tuxedo and drive across the GW Bridge in time to get my free meal with the wait staff and unlock the gorgeous grand piano. Every night I'd say hello to the bartender and after he got my confidence he pulled out his wallet and told me this story, a true tale, melodramatic but verbatim:

> *I've got two pictures of two beautiful kids in my wallet.*
> *You can tell that they're mine cuz they both look so much like me.*
> *Someone said, "Say, cheese" and they each gave a smile for the camera.*
> *There's Bobby at 4 and Chrissy the day she turned 3.*
>
> *They're my only two kids and, boy, how I really love them.*
> *I would hug 'em and never let go if they were here.*
> *These two pictures are old. I wish I could show you some new ones.*
> *They surely have changed. I haven't seen them that much this year.*
>
> *When I close up my wallet, my children are face to face,*
> *Taking a good, long look at each other.*
> *Are they trying to see what unites them as sister and brother?*
> *But they've never met and probably never will.*
>
> *Cuz one lives in New York and one lives in California*
> *With two different moms, two different hometowns far apart.*
> *But I've got a place where my two kids can be together:*
> *Face to face in my wallet and side by side in my heart.*
>   ("Two Pictures In My Wallet", 1984)

Meanwhile, Sy Rosen had been handling my taxes.

I didn't notice when a few years went by without a call from him. As it turned out, he'd met a woman and moved to a distant state with her. But first, with great elan, he lustily threw his briefcase into a lake in Central Park. For dramatic purposes, I still believe that my tax returns were in that suitcase, which (insert spooky music here) eventually led to trouble with the IRS.

After Sy rode off into the sunset with the nurse, the Second Accountant in this Tale, Sy's assistant, assured me that he could take me on and I wouldn't have to worry about a thing.

But then the ex-assistant rose in the accounting firm and got too important to do my taxes so he delegated my account to an underling who pretty much forgot about me, so that didn't work out.

Then someone recommended a firm that handled the taxes of people in The Entertainment Industry. C.C. and I ended up referring to them as "The Fox And The Snake".

They had a fancy office and berated me for not having some elaborate scheme to dodge a lot of taxes.

Virtuous to the core, I protested, "But is this legal?" They said it was 99.99% legal and besides all their clients did it and none ever got caught.

Then I got caught. Christmas Day 1985, I got a call from Internal Revenue.

It turned out there was something unholy about the scheme set up by The Fox And The Snake. The I.R.S. wanted a lot of money—NOW.

I said I didn't have it. At the time I was just a cocktail piano-player. And then, in a voice I'll never forget, like the bookie's strong-arm in a B-movie, the voice from the I.R.S. said, "Surely you know somewhere you can get it."

Without enough in the bank to cover the debt but living in a huge SoHo loft that we had put together ourselves, we knew we'd have to sell it and move.

So we sold our loft and moved to the suburbs and, ignoring the maxim that one should always keep family and finances separate, my cousin became my accountant.

And that worked out fine.

So much for maxims.

TRACK 37 – TAJ AND THE BLUES

Remember that day back in 1968 in Columbia's L.A. studios when Janis coerced me into playing piano on "Turtle Blues"—when I was as unskilled at playing The Blues as my 8 year old granddaughter would be at flying a plane.

Well, as you might recall, earlier that day I was playing piano for The Electric Flag recordings. As we were running through Bobby Hebb's song, "Sunny", and I was figuring out a piano part with my eyes on the keyboard, I looked up and there was Taj Mahal leaning over the piano. We had never met before but I certainly knew and enjoyed his first two records.

Once again McLuhan's "Medium Is the Massage" album figured in. Taj said he often listened to it and, because it was so chock-full of information, he'd put on headphones and listen to the left side of the stereo all the way through and then do the same with the right.

Two years later, in 1970, Taj called and asked me if I wanted to join his quartet for a European tour. I said I'd have to think about it.

After deliberating for 2 seconds, I said, "Yes!"

I had always wanted to go out on the road with a band and this particular offer had another plus for me.

There's always something new to learn in music and I wanted to learn The Blues.

You see, there's a five-note ("pentatonic") scale that's natural to human beings without exception around the world. If you can get to a piano, you can hear it by playing the black notes.

When you think about it, the fact that that scale is natural to human beings throughout the world is astounding. Why is that? Where did it come from?

Well, the way I figure, when the wind blew fiercely across the mouth of a cave or across an open reed, those were the notes our ancient troglodyte relatives would have heard, just as we would hear them today. They're natural harmonics. It's pretty basic.

With my work with The Band, I had become totally immersed in one of the five-note scales, that of Bluegrass melodies, the melody notes of "Old Macdonald Had A Farm".

It had become second-nature to improvise and write using that five-note scale. (If you play those five black notes on a piano, the Bluegrass five-note scale centers around the F-sharp.)

At the same time I knew intellectually what the five-note pentatonic Blues scale was. (The same five notes, but centered around E-flat, the melody of "Sometimes I Feel Like A Motherless Child"), but I had never played the Blues scale enough, never been immersed in it to the same degree. I hadn't yet "got it in my soul".

Now I had a chance to do that.

So off we went to Europe.

Beside Taj, there was bassist, Bill Rich, who sets the standard for electric bass players as far as I'm concerned, the wonderful and subtle guitarist, Jesse Edwin Davis, and drummer, Jimmy Carstein.

One person who I'll never forget was Ron Nehoda, Taj's road manager who could have worn a T-shirt that said "Mister Fun". I could never be sure how efficient he was as a road manager but he sure liked to have a good time. If there was a cliff in front of him with a woman or a party at the bottom, he would jump.

Ed Davis, a native Kiowa, was a dignified, taciturn guy. He wasn't talkative, but he was direct and to the point. And as with most musicians, his personality was reflected in his playing. His sound was easily recognizable as it is throughout Taj's first albums. The last time I saw him was at Leon Russell's birthday marathon recording session. He passed on shortly after that. Hard drugs. A great loss. Too soon.

In Bill Rich, Taj had his perfect bandmate.
Billy Rich quickly became one of my favorite people and remains a close friend whom I wish I saw more often. Nowadays as a solid third of the Taj Mahal Trio (along with drummer, Kester Smith, "Smitty"), he's on the road somewhere in the world for a good portion of the year. But with his easy laugh, sense of humor, curiosity and his plain dependability as a friend, he's hard to beat.
And as a bass player, Bill Rich is solid as a rock, always playing tasty, interesting lines and the right notes. And, to top it off, he's like a metronome. I always love playing in any band when Bill Rich is playing bass.
If you want to hear the definitive Bill Rich, listen to any recording of Taj's "Streetwalker" where Billy maintains a breathtaking, melodic, driving shuffle pattern through all the chords for sometimes 20 minutes straight. Stamina. Musicianship. Joy.

"T"   Billy

Then there's Taj himself. Traveling on buses, trains and planes through Europe, I got to know the dedicated musician, born Henry Fredericks in Springfield, Massachusetts about the same time I was born 200 miles away.

> We were driving by some pasture in the French countryside when Taj pointed out the different breeds of the cattle for me. He had considered being a veterinarian and farmer. He had started off in that direction when he had his Revelation. The affinity he'd always felt deep inside for music simply overwhelmed any more conventional plans, and the caterpillar became a Blues butterfly.

But "butterfly" couldn't be a less appropriate word for Taj in performance. Although he can sing a tender ballad, it's his runaway-train energy that comes to mind first.

Recently I sat in with the trio and there was Taj, now a senior icon of The Blues. I said to him, "Y'know, if there'd been no Taj Mahal, there would be no Keb Mo." He said, "I know. Keb Mo told me the same thing."

Back then, on the European tour, Taj wasn't playing any piano and I'm not even sure he played any guitar. But he sure played the harmonica. He had figured out a technique on the harmonica in which he would blow while blocking the holes in the middle of the instrument with his tongue, making the notes on either side of it sound. Those notes were an octave apart which made for a really powerful sound.

Our first stop in Europe, right after we got off the plane, was a TV studio in Frankfurt where the locals pronounced "Taj" to rhyme with "Bach". Our last stop before we left the continent for England was the Olympia Theatre in Paris, the scene of so many live recordings I owned, from Duke Ellington to Aretha Franklin.
The Olympia ran through acts faster than babies run through diapers. There was continuous music all day and all night long. As I recall, we performed in the middle of the afternoon.

One day on our tour bus, the conversation switched from cows to The Blues.

I'm always interested in language. In answer to "What are The Blues", the Oxford English Dictionary points out that, way back in 17th Century England, the term "blue devils" referred to hallucinations from alcohol withdrawal.

Musically speaking, "What is The Blues?" is of course a different question.

Writing a book, it's hard to guess who's reading it. For instance, if you're a musician, you know what The Blues is. But others of you might be curious to know what's behind the term. So, for those of you in the latter group,

I can try to break it down. It seems deceptively simple but I always find it interesting

A little math: The Blues is a unique song form. It's 12 bars long: a "12-bar Blues." It's made up of 3 sentences, but <u>the first two sentences are exactly the same.</u>

Are you with me so far? You can read that again. That's important.

Like :

"Oh, Baby, what you do to me.
Oh, Baby, what you do to me..."

So, since the words are the same, what makes those first 2 sentences different?
Well, the difference is a musical one: <u>the chord underneath each of those sentences is different.</u>

It was at that point in my discussion with Taj that I suddenly understood how and why that song-form solidified into the 12-Bar Blues form that has become so popular today.

When the chord under the second sentence changes, it changes <u>one single note</u> in the melody– and that tiny change of one note expresses all the pain, possibility, poignance that you now can hear in every Blues Bar, from every Blues cover band in the world.

"Wow! That's a mouthful," you say. "Could you de-obfuscate?"

OK. Let's say the first sentence, sung over both of the first two sentences, is *"Oh, Baby, what you do to me."*

The first time it's sung doesn't give the listener much information about what the singer feels.

BUT, when the chord changes for that second sentence, and <u>one note</u> in the melody changes, it gives the lyric a minor-key, sadder cast, and all of a sudden the same sentence, *"Oh, Baby, what you do to me."*, becomes ironic, darker. Not happy.

The Blues song-form then has become a vehicle to express The Blues sadness.

In our example, the singer is now telling us that whatever Baby does is, at the very least, a problem.

For instance:

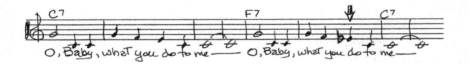

Those are the first 8 bars. The chords are written. Play this if you can and notice how the melody on the word "do" changes. Sad.

The third and last sentence of that 12-bar blues form is usually a rhyming comment on the other sentence. So the entire verse might be:

Oh, Baby, what you do to me
Oh, Baby, what you do to me
You fill my life with pain and misery.

So that's The Blues.

Back to our story.

In England with Taj, we played a couple of shows in big cities like Manchester and Liverpool before we hit London where we played the Albert Hall. (No, I never learned "how many holes it takes to fill the Albert Hall".) But, on the way to the gig, I found myself in Mick Jagger's limo with The Mick himself. He was in a jolly mood, anticipating Taj's show. After the show, it got even better. Eric Clapton invited Brooke and me back to his house in Surrey which was more like a castle. A rambling stone labyrinth which seemed as chilly as it was in the time of Henry VIII.

Eric was the most cordial of hosts. We sat around and talked into the night and at one point I mentioned that I regretted not having learned to play the guitar. He said the problem was that I hadn't had a decent guitar to learn on.

"Here," he said, "Take this." And he gave me a guitar that he said he didn't need anymore since he hadn't used it since he was in Cream.

Now, when I tell this story to guitar aficionados, they say, "Wow! Do you mean his L-500 Flying Z with the High Altitude Adapter, Overdrive and Chocolate Sauce?"

I have no idea. I am not a guitar aficionado. All I know was that I felt it must be a guitar of some significance and so I attempted to decline the gift.

But Eric, gracious soul that he is, insisted I take it and, the next morning, put it in the "boot" (that's the trunk) of his car before his man drove us back to London.

When we arrived at our hotel I told his man to leave it in the boot, that I couldn't possibly take it. What if I never learned to play the guitar? It would be a waste.

At this point, the aforementioned guitar aficionados invariably beat their heads against the wall at my apparent idiocy and lack of foresight.

✳ ✳ ✳

There would be more tours with Taj.

A couple of years later, a call came from Ron Nehoda, "Mister Fun".

Taj was putting together a tour, this time in the U.S. and with horns. We called it the Tuba Band for short.

The horns were being assembled by my old friend and senior by 4 days, Howard Johnson, and Taj asked me to assemble a rhythm section.

Of course Bill Rich would be the bass player. But with Ed Davis gone to That Big Jam Session In The Sky and no drummer on board, I decided on John Hall and Greg Thomas.

> I can pinpoint this in my memory as 1972 because, when we got together in Woodstock for a few weeks of rehearsal, there was Bill Rich, and I had just received the first test pressing of my first album. He and I listened to it and he gave me the best compliment I could ever receive: "Play it again."

Howard's horn section was recruited from his all-tuba band, either called "Sub-structure" or "Gravity" at the time: Bob Stewart, Joe Daley and Earl McIntyre.

We played some East Coast dates culminating at the Fillmore East. I remember seeing Clive Davis backstage in a black mink coat. Leon Russell opened the bill and we followed.

> Before we went on, there was Stevie Wonder backstage too. Ron Nehoda, always the prankster, must have told him that Taj's whole band was black before he brought Stevie over to me and Stevie whispered in my ear that he'd had enough of Leon's white band and was looking forward to hearing us play.

(The Fillmore concert led to the only other recorded piano performance of mine that embarrasses me, beside "Turtle Blues".

One of the songs we did, "Ain't Gonna Whistle Dixie No More", had very very very long solos, mine being no exception. At the actual concert I started off gradually and finally built to some kind of overdone frantic climax.

BUT ... Dave Rubinson , who produced the recording, decided to edit my solo and just use the end of it. So, on the record, there's no subtle preparation for the frantic climax. The frantic climax just comes out of nowhere after which Taj yells my name.

Justice would have been better served if he'd yelled Dave's name.)

We took some time off after those East Coast shows and then regrouped on the West Coast for some more rehearsals before embarking on a tour of the rest of the country. But this time John Hall and Greg Thomas had been replaced by Hoshal Wright and Jimmy Otie.

Hoshal was a running buddy of Bill Rich from Omaha and a very funny guy whose wisecracks kept me in stitches. I remember him referring to his kids as Curtain Crawlers and Crumb Crushers. He was a fine guitar player too.

Jimmy Otie came to us fresh from Little Richard's band and was full of tales that I could <u>never</u> print here ...

Well, ... O.K.

He said Richard dressed the guys in his band in skin-tight white pants with no underwear. "So the women can see the print o' yo' dick".

Ah, show bizness.

Now that—from Jimmy, in his Southern drawl—is clearly merely Hearsay. And doesn't jibe with the fact that Little Richard became a preacher. It's not very preacher-ly instruction.

But one thing Jimmy told me is PG rated. It's musical and it's something that I often do: often a song will end with 2 chords, the chords that generally support the word, "Amen". Musicians call them the "four chord" followed by the "one chord" or, classically a "plagal cadence".

He told me that his Sunday school teacher used to prolong that four chord over and over, teasing the listener who can't wait for it to resolve to the one chord. Sort of like "A-a-a-a-a-a-men". It's a lot of fun and I do it now a lot.

In this band I was "the rice in the raisins". Unless I happened to pass by a mirror, I saw nothing but black folks and I never felt out of place or different.
I remember the on-the-road camaraderie of us all, walking through anonymous airports with Howard leading us scat-singing "Way Back Home" by The Jazz Crusaders.

In 1971, Black Power had captured a lot of attention. Nothing was made of my skin color on tours– with one single exception.

One night we shared a bill with a black artist who shot me a look that would have withered the entire tulip output of Holland: Miles Davis.

And how ironic that I was so close to one of his best friends and collaborators: Gil Evans.

TRACK 38 – THE MUSIC COMMITTEE

I can track my early interest in jazz because it paralleled the development of the music itself.

At first it was Dixieland: Louis Armstrong and New Orleans. Then my tastes, paralleling the history of jazz itself, went up the Mississippi River to Chicago and the groups that Eddie Condon led. Then that shining son of Chicago, Benny Goodman and the recording I had of his 1938 Carnegie Hall concert. And the other big bands: the Duke and the Count. And the piano players: Art Tatum, Errol Garner. Then bebop: Charlie Parker. And the great horn soloists: Coleman Hawkins, Bud Shank, J.J. Johnson, Clifford Brown, Ben Webster, Chet Baker. And then Dave Brubeck, whom I tried to emulate in high school in my thick horn-rims.

But ever since I was about thirteen and in one band or another, I was the arranger for that band.

So I listened carefully and learned from the work of a lot of great arrangers: Sy Oliver, Duke, Billy Strayhorn and the guys who wrote for Basie: Neil Hefti, Ernie Wilkins, Quincy Jones. The West Coast guys like Shorty Rogers, Gerry Mulligan, J.J. Johnson, Pete Rugolo.

I'm leaving a lot of gifted arrangers out but the one who stood apart because of the colors he could draw from the same instruments everyone else was using was Gil.

Gil Evans had started out in the Big Band era writing most notably for the Claude Thornhill band. But he really came to the attention of jazz-heads with the famous Birth of the Cool sessions, a recording of less than 10 songs by a band of less than 10 players put together by Miles Davis. Gerry Mulligan, John Lewis, Johnny Carisi, Lee Konitz, George Wallington and others were part of the project. And so was Gil.

Maybe the time Miles and Gil spent working together in that period was what inspired them to collaborate on several albums for Columbia years later with a large jazz orchestra—"Miles Ahead", "Porgy and Bess" and most significantly "Sketches of Spain".
If any of you reading this have never heard "Sketches Of Spain", put this book down right now, find that recording, get comfortable and listen to it.

I'll wait.

Cut to 1976.

C.C. and I had moved to NYC and were looking for a school for our kids. We had intended to enroll them in public school but that was suddenly a bad idea that year because of a NYC teachers' strike. We came across a progressive school in our neighborhood called City and Country.

The school gave us the opportunity to minimize the considerable private school tuition for two kids in New York City by letting us barter with services. C.C. was asked if she would coach some kids in acting and mime and I was asked if I would serve on the school's "music committee". They said there was one other parent on that committee and his name was Gil Evans.

Hard to believe my good fortune. This guy had been my musical idol for years and here we were together on this little committee.

The school put together a fund-raising day in the spring and, along with a bake sale and games for the kids (mostly involving balloons), they turned one classroom into a "coffee house" and asked me to provide some live music.

I hefted my 2 ton Fender Rhodes electric piano into the classroom and got my friend, Tony Coniff, to join me on bass.

I got absorbed in playing my original compositions and my eyes were on the keyboard, just as they were when I looked up at that Electric Flag session some years earlier and had discovered Taj Mahal listening intently. But this time, when I looked up, there was Gil, 12 inches away from the piano listening in rapt attention with his eyes closed and, barely perceptibly, moving to the music. Whoa! Was I thrilled! Here was a musician whose music and taste I respected at the top of my Respect List listening to my music and taste.

And we began a deep friendship.

I was following the progress of Gil's new big band and got them a deal to record a live concert, released as an album titled "Priestess".

I brought Gil to Albert's attention and, since Robbie was aware of Gil too, Albert offered to lend Gil some needed support.

Y'see, in spite of having made some of the most famous jazz records in history, Gil, like all arrangers, received no royalties from the sales of records. Artists did. Composers did. Producers did. But arrangers did not.

One day, in the heart of Manhattan on a break from mixing "Priestess", Gil and I sat on the stone border of a flower bed in front of a steel-and-glass office building, engaged in unhurried conversation.
None of the NYC lunch-timers rushing around us in a blur knew who he was. None stopped to reward him with a thank you for his gifts to the art of music, just as the royalty set-up in the record business offered him no reward.

Gil told me that if he had known when he started out that arrangers faced such dismal pecuniary prospects, he would've chosen a different profession.

That would've been a great loss!

TRACK 39: SHORT STORIES

I've had the good fortune to work with a lot of wonderful and interesting people. There are so many talented artists "out there" and whether or not they acquire the audience numbers they deserve depends a lot on luck, good or bad.

In this section, I've picked out a few, not because they're more talented than the rest but because I can tell a story around each of them.

Gil Evans from the preceding chapter figures in David Sanborn's story, so I'll start with Dave.

David Sanborn and I knew each other from Woodstock when he had been a member of Paul Butterfield's Blues Band.

Dave played on one my own albums. I wrote an exultant horn chart for a song called "Open Up, Summertime". He seemed to just eat up the part I wrote for his alto.

Even though he doesn't solo, in the ensemble you can recognize his sound (like Janis' sound standing out in the midst of the background vocals of Big Brother.). Maybe it was Dave's stint with Butterfield's band or maybe it came earlier, but Dave "sings" through his horn like a soulful vocalist. He's not just playing notes. He was the first to play with that identifiable tone but quickly other sax players were copying him faster than teenagers ape the styles of their idols .

On that session, I was out in the studio while we were recording some takes with the players and I called into the booth for the engineer, Phil Ramone, to change to a new reel of tape. I had spent so much time in the studio by then that I was subconsciously logging how much music we had put on the 20 minute reel and I knew that we'd need to open up a new one. My experience in the studio, as it was embodied in that incident, impressed Dave. He told me that he decided then that I was the right guy to produce an album for him.

Working with him was fun. Dave's a smart cookie.

Besides finally getting some public acclaim, Dave was a highly respected player among New York musicians. So a lot of great players were eager to work on his album.

A few of the players were fueled by cocaine, which had supplanted marijuana among some (though not me) as the drug-of-choice around that time, 1979. So the sessions would often go on and on until dawn.

I didn't understand why Dave would play a magnificent solo during an overdub session, and then always, always, always want to do one more – until Gil Evans, in his wisdom said, "Of course he would. He's playing a wonderful instrument, into a wonderful microphone, wearing wonderful headphones through which he hears wonderful musicians backing him up. Why wouldn't he want to keep on doing that?"

* * *

<u>John Hartford</u> grew up in St. Louis and was such a Mississippi River enthusiast that he actually got a license to pilot a Mississippi steamboat. But my connection with him was musical.

He was a very talented multi-instrumentalist and song-writer who had written "Gentle On My Mind" which was a big hit for Glen Campbell. He was a regular on The Smothers Brothers TV show.

He came to Woodstock in 1972 companioned with guitarist Norman Blake to make a bluegrass album but he needed a bass player. We were driving through town at the time so I pointed out a fellow who crossed in front of the car carrying his laundry to the laundromat.

"There's one of the best bass players in the world", I said. It was my friend Dave Holland, who had played with Miles Davis. We stopped Dave and asked if he wanted to play on a bluegrass record.

"What's bluegrass?" asked Dave, born and raised in England.

"Well, it's like jazz, only from Appalachia."

We made a wonderful album called Morning Bugle. Just John, Norman and Dave. Hartford didn't want to hear playbacks because he felt they broke the flow for the musicians. And he was right.

John was an easy guy to get along with – a prince.

***

In 1978 an independent record company called Tomato Records asked me to produce a cowboy singer/poet named Gary McMahan from Greeley Colorado. Gary was the real deal. Wrangled horses and spit tobacco. Plus he was a clever, witty guy and fun to be around.

One of my favorite poems of his contains the lines:

"When I die I want to be made into a saddle
that a beautiful woman will buy
so that I can be between the 2 things I love the most."

Gary now.   Gary as he imagines his future self.

* * *

By 1993 exec Ron Goldstein had left Warners to become the head of Private Music, a label owned by Chris Blackwell, famed as the head of Island Records, and now Ron asked me to produce a piano-playing songwriter, <u>A.J. Croce</u>, Jim Croce's son.

Now I had shied away from producing piano-players because I'm a piano player myself and I felt I could contribute more to an artist whose orientation was not piano-based.

> That's probably a rationalization; more to the point would be that I felt I'd be envious, sitting on my hands while the artist was doing what I wanted to be doing.
> I had earlier turned down Bruce Lundvall's offer to produce Billy Joel for that reason.

But with A.J. I dispensed with that envy forever because I realized that A.J. was the same age as my youngest daughter whom I always helped out in any way that I could. So I transferred that warmth to A.J.'s project.

He turned out to be a wonderful interesting guy. His mom, Ingrid, ran a famous restaurant in San Diego called "Croce's" that served great food and had a very active music room. It was here that young A.J. had cut his performing teeth.

> A.J. had trouble seeing. I don't know the definition of legally blind but, riding as a passenger in his car was a leap of faith. He asked me to read those big green freeway signs for him. You might ask how he got his license. A.J. and "Croce's" were very popular in San Diego. I'm not sure they even made him take a driving test.

***

And <u>Hirth Martinez</u>.
Hirth passed away while I was compiling this memoir.

He began life as Samuel Martinez.
But, as a fledgling musician in a world whose biases cannot be denied, he de-hispanisized himself a bit and made up the name, Robert Hirth. I have no idea why he settled on the name "Hirth." But later, when he decided to embrace his roots, some folks already knew him as Hirth so "Hirth Martinez" became his moniker.

> He had come to me in a round-about way, but I'm so glad he did. Hirth was singing some of his far-out lyrics in a guitar shop in California when Bob Dylan happened by and heard him. Bob recommended him to Robbie Robertson who produced Hirth's first album. Then Robbie recommended me to do his second.

We recorded it in the studio The Band owned in Zuma Beach. (It had formerly been the residence of the equine TV star, Mr. Ed. Only in Hollywood would a TV star who was a horse have his own house!)

And Hirth was a lovely person. He was a fine musician. Easy to get along with. An easy laugher. An appreciator of the best of his peers, generous in his praise. Of all those artists I produced, I can't think of any that was more pleasant to hang out with than Hirth.

Hirth was a champ.

* * *

Fran and Jay Landesman were wonderful, vibrant characters from the Beatnick/Bopster Age, a generation before mine. They had owned a club in St. Louis called The Crystal Palace where Barbra Streisand, Lenny Bruce, Woody Allen and Maya Angelou appeared before they were "Somebody".

At one point in the Fifties, they simply gave up on America and re-established themselves in London where their house in Islington became a salon for the wilder British show biz types and any hip American acts breezing through town.

Fran wrote the lyrics for some enduring jazz standards like "Spring Can Really Hang You Up The Most" and "The Ballad Of The Sad Young Men".

Fran   Jay

Jay was an incredible character. His autobiography is entitled "Rebel Without Applause". He was always at the exciting heart of anything new, whether it was the Beat Generation and Allen Ginsberg in the U.S. or later, "Swinging London" and Yoko Ono. A man with a way with words he glamorized defeat with the slogan "Let's take the joy out of success and put the fun back in failure."

I wrote some songs with Fran and, in the course of that, I met Larry Coleman, a publisher with The Richmond Organization. I'm going to bring in Larry here because he told me a good personal story.

> He was a hapless soldier in the Pacific during World War II. His unit had met no resistance occupying a particular lonely island. With nothing much going on, one day alone on a beach, he discovered a pump organ and then got so swept away in the music he was making that he didn't notice the Japanese soldiers who snuck up and surrounded him and then put him in a P.O.W. camp. Music had truly transported him.

We became real tight with jazz vocalists Jackie and Roy, or, as it said on their wedding certificate, Jackie Cain and Roy Kral.

We loved them and would have dinners together at each other's houses and laugh far into the night.

And I helped them with 2 of their last albums.

Some of their family's history has edged into the everyday language of our family and lodged there—a non-denominational pre-meal grace: "Blessings On The Meal" and the word, "hode".

> One of their daughters, a 2 year old at the time, had heard her parents repeatedly referring to someone as an "asshole", but all she picked up was "hode". So that became our word for a generic jerk.

> "What a hode!"

***

I really can't call this a complete memoir without mentioning 3 other fine artists whose albums I produced, Rachel Faro, Michael Franks and Pierce Turner.

I first heard Rachel (born Carol Miller, presently calling herself Nirmala when I met her) in Cyrus Faryar's kitchen in LA. Her big, full voice knocked me out and it wasn't long before I realized what a gifted songwriter she was as well. She made a fine album called "Refugees".

I was delighted at the prospect of working with Michael Franks on his "Tiger In The Rain" album because he was giving me carte blanche with the arrangements and much of his music had a Brazilian bossa nova flavor, an idiom I had come to love. Because some of his other tunes leaned toward rock, we used 2 rhythm sections, a rock one and with a Brazilian cast. This album is one of my faves.

I helped Irish singer/songwriter Pierce Turner with his album, "Now Is Heaven". I learned a lot working with him. He was very adventurous in the instrumentation he envisioned for his project. Though Celtic music is in evidence in some of the instruments and the singers, there's a lot of synth in there too. For instance the voices and dark instrumental colors he chose for "Smokestack View really evoke a factory town. When you hear it you feel like you have to brush the soot off your shoulders.

TRACK 40 – "JACKRABBITT SLIM"

Steve Forbert gets a chapter of his own because I have 3 Forbert stories that I will trot out.

Story #1:

1979. Nat Weiss, who had brought the demo of "Red Rubber Ball" to me way back when – which had ultimately catapulted both of us up onto the next level of our careers – called me on a Friday to say that he had a new artist, Steve Forbert, who was about to cut an album in Nashville.

> He was calling because a producer (whom we shall refer to as "Mr. My-Word-Is-Gold") had been signed to record Steve but had just told Nat that Barbra Streisand wanted him to work with her ASAP.
> He assured Nat that he was a man who honored his previous commitments ("My word is gold"). But, wouldn'tcha know it, on Monday I was on a plane for Nashville to take over the Forbert project that Mr. My-Word-Is-Gold abandoned.

Mr. My-Word-Is-Gold had hired the cream of Nashville's players for the week of recording. But after the first day, Steve seemed uneasy and he told me they weren't right for his music.

Uh-oh.

Those Nashville stars had already been hired and besides, since I didn't work much in that town, no replacements came to mind.

Back in my hotel room, realizing that things had gotten out of control (not my favorite condition), I picked up the only book around, the bible which the Gideons had left there for just such situations, and I opened it at random. My eye fell upon a Psalm in the middle of the book that began, "To The Chief Musician".

"Well, "I thought, "That's appropriate. I'm the chief musician on this gig."

"Hold on a minute there, Buster", said a voice that came from somewhere and nowhere at the same time. And I realized that King James's scribes were not referring to me but to some force greater than I, greater than Steve, greater than the entire city of Nashville. So I said, "Okay, Chief Musician, you've got this one." And I went to sleep.

> flocks; the valleys also are covered
> over with corn; they shout for
> joy, they also sing.
>
> ### PSALM 66
> To the chief Musician, A Song *or* Psalm.
>
> MAKE a joyful noise unto God, all ye lands:
> 2 Sing forth the honour of his

Note to self: you are not the Chief Musician.

The next morning, word came that Nashville's Finest had independently decided they weren't right for Steve's project. They would leave without expecting to be paid for the week they had been booked AND they recommended some terrific younger players who filled the bill very nicely indeed thank you.

So there we were, ready to go.

Story #2:

I will always have the greatest respect for Steve's songwriting chops. Listen to "Sadly Like A Soap Opera" or "Make It All So Real" from that album.
And I was on the same page as he when it came to his insistence on "keeping it real."

In this case, he wanted "Jackrabbitt Slim" to be an album that was recorded totally live.

A test case came up right away. We recorded a take on the first song and then listened to a playback in the control room. It was wonderful but Mike Leach, the bass player, said, "I flubbed one note. Let me go in and fix it."

"Uh-uh", said Steve, "Let's all go in and do it again."

And that was the way the album went: totally, honestly live, no overdubs, no splices. Not one.

And this was with a LOT of players. All live. In the same room at the same time: Steve, singing, playing harmonica and guitar, another guitar player, piano, bass, drums, organ (doubling on accordion), 3 horns and 3 additional vocalists. And the engineer, Gene Eichelberger did a wonderful job capturing a certain transparency through which you could hear each of the elements clearly.

But ... (must there always be a "but"?) ...

The 3rd story:

Steve, for all his smarts, his songwriting and performing talent, can overthink things, and he will admit that.

I brought those wonderful, pristine tapes to the mastering room in NYC where I would be meeting Steve to lock in the final audio aspect of the recordings and Steve showed up with the new Rolling Stones album and said, "I want our album to sound as hot as this."

Well, ... no. This was not a case of apples and oranges. This was a case of delicate birdsong at dawn versus an explosion at a munitions plant.

The Stones' album had been recorded one-instrument-at-a-time with each element maximized so that everything was "in your face" – every element at top volume all the way. Our album "breathed". You felt like you were privileged to be in the room while this fine musical event was occurring.

The Customer Is Always Right so that's the way "Jackrabbitt Slim" was released: bird calls from a 500 pound seagull.

TRACK 41 – THE LAST WALTZ

As I wrote earlier, my dad had forgone a career as a professional musician, but music was in his bones.

He became one of the founders of the Norwalk Symphony and, as a little kid, I often sat in the middle of that huge orchestra during rehearsals. And there I learned something obvious: what was going on there was definitely NOT a democracy.

There were almost 80 people in the orchestra. Can you imagine the confusion there would be if it were a democracy?

I quickly got it that things were organized more along the lines of a military chain of command.

The conductor, of course, is the general, who takes his marching orders from the composer. But all of the musicians, from the best to the worst, know that part of their job is to concede all authority to the conductor. They don't find that their liberty has been squelched. They're happy to do that. It's expected of them. Being a good follower is part of the gig.

So, at a young age, watching grade school band directors and symphony orchestra conductors, I saw how efficiently that arrangement worked and I felt that I myself would some day be capable of standing up in front of an orchestra, leading a bunch of talented, tractable players toward a fulfilling musical result. As soon as I got a chance, I was eager to assume that role.

It's what lit my fire through the bands I led in high school, through the shows I conducted in college, through the recording sessions I ran.

And it was especially useful when I was asked to be the Musical Director of The Last Waltz.

Early in the fall of 1976, Robbie Robertson called me to ask me to be the Musical Director for this mega-concert he had in mind.
What did that mean? Well, my title could've been "wrangler".

The plan was that The Band would back up all of these different artists but, apart from Garth, the other guys in The Band didn't read music so I would have to explain to them in their terms what to play – what chords, what the format of the songs were, what notes made up particular lines in the arrangement, etc.

So, that fall, they flew me out to the studio in Zuma Beach that they'd been using (the equine Mr. Ed's old house if you recall) And it was there that we spent a week preparing for the concert.

It all went pretty smoothly. Each day one or two artists would show up to rehearse their numbers.

Muddy, Joni, Van
Clapton, Ronnie, Bobby Charles
Mac, Butter, Dylan

The way we worked on Van Morrison's song, "Caravan" was typical. I wrote the chord names out on paper for Rick, Robbie and Richard. Then, by the time they were on stage for the show, I had it down to hand signals: 3 fingers held horizontally reminded them that an E chord was coming up, etc.

When Joni Mitchell rehearsed her songs with us, I couldn't for the life of me, identify the strange and wonderful chords she was playing. Even when I looked at the hand formations she was using on the neck of the guitar, it was a mystery.

So I asked her.

She said, "Sometimes I feel that I know too much about music so I'll tune my guitar to some random tunings JUST TO MAKE MYSELF STUPID."

I loved that.

But the best rehearsal of all was the dress rehearsal at Winterland. There I was in the middle of the empty hall feeling like the ringleader at a circus calling the shots for an audience of, basically, me.

The afternoon of the show Robbie asked me what I was going to wear. I was so excited about the upcoming show that I hadn't given it much thought but, since I was going to conduct the horns and play the piano for the few tunes that were too tough for Richard, I had to go downtown to Macy's and buy a jacket.

I found one that I liked. It looked like it may have come from a Central American Indian jacket maker. It wasn't formal at all. It was colorful. I liked it. I bought it.

Robbie saw it and said, "You're not going to wear <u>that</u>?" (I would have stood out too much I suppose.) So Garth lent me a black leather jacket and that was that.

My taste.

Garth's taste.
(reflecting the taste of
a nephew of an undertaker,
which he was.)

The night of the show, when I got to the Winterland ballroom at around 6 o'clock, it took my breath away.

> Things had already been in full swing for a couple of hours. Complete turkey dinners had been served to over 5000 people, most of whom were dressed in special finery, many women in floor length gowns.
>
> And people were dancing. Not disco, not a mosh pit, but Strauss waltzes played by a large orchestra.

Winterland had been decorated in a style you could call Nouveau classy Viennese with potted palms and hedges brought in, along with chandeliers and a set onstage borrowed from the San Francisco Opera.

I went backstage to check in on the artists who were about to take part in this memorable show.

It should be said that the drug-du-jour at that time was cocaine.

> Someone told me that cocaine was part of the regular rations for the German army during World War II to make them energetic and compliant soldiers.

Energy and compliance turned out to be the perfect recipe for this bunch of musicians at The Last Waltz concert.

I myself kept my nose clean. I could see that someone had to stay focused, clear and in charge.

And that turned out to be a good thing:
When The Band finally went on, I listened to the first songs from the sound board out in the middle of the hall to make sure that the balance between the instruments coming through the sound system was as good as it could be.
Then came the first number with the horns who had been added to the concert. I went up onstage to make sure all was OK. And that was a stroke of luck
I stood by the horn section as they came out and took their places in front of their music stands.
Robbie turned to us and began to count off the next song. "1-2-3-"
Wait a minute! Something's wrong. That tempo is way too fast for the song that the horn players have on their music stands.

Yikes! Hold it!
I stuck my hand out in Robbie's direction with the intensity of the Supremes' "Stop In The Name Of Love".
The sequence had been changed and nobody had told the horn section.
So things stopped for a few minutes while the horn players rearranged their music in the revised order.

That part's not in the movie.

It turned out that Robbie had written a "Last Waltz Theme" prior to the concert. When The Band left the stage for a break, he sprung it on me, and I taught it to anyone who needed to know it during the long intermission.

After the concert was over, Dylan's "people" stormed the remote recording truck where Elliott Mazer was getting the concert down on tape and they grabbed the tapes of the songs Bob sang on, in order to have control over Bob's part of the show.

Later, there was a cast-and-friends-only jam session in the basement of the hotel. I remember how wonderful Muddy Waters was, how Dr. John fit right in with him and I remember rock critic Robert Palmer pulling a tin whistle out of his pocket and joining in.

When it came time to put together an album of the concert, Robbie brought in Rob Fraboni to help him out in California while I worked back in NYC.

Robbie realized that there were not many people of color nor women in the concert. So, he added some performers to the movie who were not at the live show: The Staple Singers and Emmylou Harris recorded later on a soundstage with a lot of dry-ice smoke.

It also turned out that a lot of the original performances, though they made the audience happy, needed to be fixed for the record. Rick's bass was generally out of tune, Richard hit a lot of the cracks between the piano keys, Garth always looked for opportunities to improve his parts and Robbie was a perfectionist who wanted to fix his parts too. In addition, the horns, mixed in the remote truck, were badly balanced. So everyone re-did their parts—except for Levon.

All in all The Last Waltz was a glorious, ambitious scheme and I applaud The Band, Robbie in particular, Martin Scorsese, Bill Graham and all the musicians and crew who pulled it off. Some people say that it's The Best Rock Concert Movie Ever.

But... Truth, Lie or Hearsay?

Well, there's some untruth in the movie. I like to compare it to the movie, "Some Like It Hot".

In that film, we see Marilyn Monroe, Jack Lemmon and Tony Curtis playing their instruments but we know that they're not really playing. At the same time, the music we hear, played by studio musicians is terrific. We don't mind that lie at all. No harm done.

Well, the Last Waltz is the same thing. If you watch the movie carefully, you can see that the moving mouths don't always match the voices we hear and the same goes for the fingers on the guitar fingerboard. But so what? We love the movie.

But, in The Last Waltz, unlike in "Some Like It Hot", those folks we see on the screen are the same people who, later on in a recording studio, recorded some of the music we hear. So the impression that the Last Waltz was a totally live recording may be a lie, but it's just fine.

After all, it's not a film OF a concert. It's a film ABOUT a concert.

***

Hearsay: that Neil Young onstage had more white stuff on his upper lip than Santa Claus after drinking a vanilla milkshake. I didn't notice. My son, Max, says that a floating matte was used in the editing of the film to hide the fact.

My favorite Neil Young story incidentally (also hearsay) was that once, at a concert, he began with 30 minutes of material from his new album, "Tonight's The Night", which prompted someone in the audience to yell, "Play something we've heard before!" So he repeated the last song.

I love that.

The Band broke up after The Last Waltz. Or maybe even before. Why? Each of them probably had a different reason. But one thing seems to be universal in break-ups of pop groups: when one member rises up out of the group to a position of prominence, the others may feel resentment which can lead to a host of deteriorating personal results.

In the case of Robbie and The Band, as with Janis and Big Brother, one individual became separate from the pack. What had started out in a spirit of camaraderie, with shared highs and lows, now lost that communal feeling.

In Robbie's case, he had plans beyond The Band and it turned out that replacing Levon as Leader of the group had inadvertently become a stepping-stone along the way.

On the other hand, I don't think Janis ever wanted to be the Leader; it was public adulation that separated her from her fellows by making her a Star.

(Robbie never became a Star after The Band broke up; that distinction was to be Levon's.)

But Levon made no bones about his resentment toward Robbie. You couldn't speak Robbie's name around Levon.

(For all his Southern Charm, Levon could really hold a grudge. Sometimes I joked with him that he was mostly still pissed about the outcome of the Civil War.)

Central to Levon's hard feelings was his dispute with Robbie about song authorship and royalties.

In a nutshell:

> They were each holding up different models. Robbie's was the classic, ASCAP model: the writers of the music and lyrics own the copyright and receive the royalties.

> Levon was influenced by a more recent model, one that was prevalent in a lot of fledgling rock and roll acts.
> Songwriters in those bands would show up in the studio with their songs only in fragmentary form. (That wasn't the case with The Band.) Then the other players in the group would contribute a little bit, often only their own parts, and claim partial authorship for their efforts. But what those players did is <u>not</u> writing. Writing is the creating of melody and lyrics.
> But, disregarding the accepted definition, the names of everyone in the group would sometimes appear on the copyright.

> And, in addition, Levon felt that Robbie had been using Levon's personal life-experiences as grist for his writing mill and he wasn't being paid for that.
> Well, it's not unusual at all for a writer to do that.

> And, though I completely understand and sympathize with Levon's anger about it, all in all I have to side with Robbie on the traditional definition of authorship.

TRACK 42 – THE RECONSTITUTED BAND

"Click"

The sound was unmistakable. I'd heard it in so many movies.

It was pitch black. I was alone, lying on a sleeping bag on the hard floor of the upper reaches of a large barn where later, on legendary Saturday nights, crowds that taxed the tolerance of the fire marshal would strain to catch a glimpse of players down below whose music set their bodies rocking and swaying.

The floor creaked. My mind raced. It could only be one thing. I took a chance:

"Levon?"

It was him at his craziest. He'd forgotten that I had crashed there that night in his barn in between recording sessions and, with a gun in his hand, he had sensed an intruder.

It was 1992, 15 years since the break-up of The Band. Levon had retired to his house in Woodstock, a converted barn that was 25% living quarters and 75% music room. So many musicians recount the same story of Levon's kitchen hospitality.

"Lemme getcha a coke."

He'd pour you one from a bottle into a glass and the fat-chewing would start. The dialogue would change. But those Coca-Cola bottles were always there.

He had put together several ensembles including The RCO All-Stars (pronounced "Our Company") and then, finally around 1990, he re-constituted 'The Band" under that name, which Robbie had allowed the remaining members to use.

The sessions would be held, of course, in Levon's barn with Chris Andersen doing most of the engineering and occasionally Garth's right-hand engineer, Aaron Hurwitz too.

The idea of doing this album was both a turn-on and a challenge for me. Could we make a good album without Robbie's leadership? Richard had died and his absence would be strongly felt, but Levon, Rick and Garth were still on the scene and the other players were worthy substitutes.

Then Levon told me he had enough of playing with Rick's melodic bass playing and craved a steady, more conventional player. So Rob Leon, a Woodstock fixture, would play most of the bass parts on the album.

Stan Szelest, a pianist they had all known from the Ronnie Hawkins days, had taken over at the keyboard but then, ironically, he too died – shortly before the recording sessions—so Richard Bell, also a Hawkins alumnus, took his place.

Jim Weider had already replaced Robbie as the principal guitarist And Levon brought in Randy Ciarlante as a second drummer, in order to allow himself the freedom to sometimes play mandolin or guitar.

Garth, of course, remained.

So that was the new band: Levon, sometimes Rick (mostly Rob), Garth, Jimmy, Randy and Richard. Plus quite a few guest performers.

Rick, Richard Bell, Garth, Randy Ciarlante, Jim Weider, Levon. The Re-constituted Band.

The last time I worked on a Band album I was lucky to have those great songs by Robbie and Richard as raw material. This time that wouldn't be the case. But I was excited at the possibility of looking anywhere and everywhere for good songs to do.

> They had already recorded Levon singing a great version of Springsteen's "Atlantic City as part of an earlier attempt to make the album. That set a high standard.
> I told artists I knew that we were doing the record and on the hunt for songs and Artie Traum gave us a great, moody song called "Amazon" that Rick sang.
> Songwriter Joe Flood got wind of our song-search and brought the humorous "Move To Japan." I tinkered with his lyrics a little and Levon sang it.
> There still remained a great sadness over Richard's death and so we decided to include his posthumous, Ray Charles-inflected vocal on "Country Boy" and a beautiful, touching obituary that Jules Shear wrote called "Too Soon Gone".
> Altogether it was a real interesting selection of material.

The album would eventually be titled "Jericho" and, in spite of the obstacles involved in the making of the album, like my almost being shot in the middle of the night, I would call it a success.

> Levon and I had our differences of opinion. But a couple of years later, my phone rang in the middle of the night and it was Levon who wanted to affirm that, as far as he was concerned, he and I were always good friends.
> A simple call but one that meant a lot to me.

Here's a story from those sessions that has happened so many times in studios around the world that it's worth mentioning here.

> Jimmy Weider, like many guitar players, was a collector as well. When he showed up to overdub a solo on the song, "Remedy" which he co-wrote, he brought along half a dozen guitars and amps to try.

I took a deep breath. I wasn't looking forward to this.

So I said, "Look, Jimmy, right now choose the guitar you think would be best and the amp you think would be best. Then try as hard as you can to play the best solo you can." Reluctantly he narrowed down his choices and played a fine solo. I said "OK, now I'm going away for a couple of hours. The studio is yours. Try as many guitars and amps as you'd like and I'll hear a fabulous solo when I get back."

Well, you know the end of this story: The original solo was the one.

What's that saying from some Buddhist sage? First Thought, Best Thought.

TRACK 43 – THE DREAM

In 1972, when C.C. and I were first "keeping company"—a lovely phrase I first heard used by guitarist Vinnie Bell—a friend gave us the use of his beach house after the tourist season had ended.

The weather was still warm and CC strolled to the beach while I took a nap.

And I had this dream.

> In the dream I woke from my nap and went to the beach to join her. But, to my horror, there putting the make on her something fierce was this muscle-bound Adonis who looked like he could snap my gangly frame in two.
> Impulsively, the words tumbled out of my mouth, "Hey! That's my woman!"
>
> "Oh, yeah? I challenge you to a duel for her. You can pick the weapons, Skinny."
>
> "Okay," I said, "I pick spelling."
>
> At first caught off guard, he collected himself and said, "I challenge you first. Spell antidisestablishmentarianism."—a word he'd probably heard about in third grade as reportedly the longest word in the English language.
>
> "A-N-T-I- (etc.)", I spelled, "Do you want the definition as well?"

"No. Didja spell it right?"

"Yes. My turn. Pleasant."

And, as I predicted, he stumbled over the "a-n-t" at the end.

"I won," I said, clutching my Beloved whose adoring expression had "My Hero" written all over it.

"Hey, how come you're so good?", asked the brute.

"Well," said I, "I happen to be a Dictionary Repairman."

That dream attests to my love of language. And that, coupled with a lot of musical training, would make me at least an <u>appreciator</u> of song, and ultimately a song<u>writer</u> too as it turned out.

In Woodstock, the percentage of local songwriters was astoundingly high and most of them didn't have many opportunities for their work to be heard. But still they kept writing songs, and they still do to this day. Writing and writing and writing, still without the success they hope for, frustrated but still bravely scribbling away.

Why do we all do that? It's hard not to. That creative urge is monstrous, both in size and, sadly, self-delusion.

When I moved up here to my house-in-the-country, a neighbor who could be comprehensively described as "a farm woman" told me that, in response to an ad in the back of a fan magazine, she had sent her songs to "Nashville, Tennessee" and she was confident that great things would come of that.

I myself am no different, in that I am in the thrall of Creativity and undoubtably will remain so as long as I live.

But I never thought I'd make a <u>record</u> on my own. My ambitions lay at the door of any Broadway producer who would "let me" write a musical. After writing those two musicals in high school and three in college (and learning a lot in the process) I had kept my hand in while I was producing records.

Then one day, at home, I played a few songs for Paul Simon. And out of his mouth came a short sentence that put me on the road to both fulfillment and frustration.

"John," he said, " you're an artist."

Uh-oh. Please, no! <u>Not</u> a "singer/songwriter"!

(The other day I heard someone define singer/songwriters as "cry-babies". That's mean, but it's a funny line.)

I've never considered myself a singer. When I open my mouth to sing, the note I hear is not what I wanted and there's that split-second when my good sense of pitch tells my inaccurate vocal cords to slide up or down to the <u>true</u> pitch that I had been trying my darndest to hit.

I envied Robbie Robertson for having those three great singers in The Band and not having to sing himself.

Whenever I thought about writing Broadway musicals, well, I wouldn't have to sing then either. That would be a good thing.

But, with Paul's imprimatur and my considerable ego, the road to doing a singer/songwriter album loomed in front of me like an empty twelve-lane freeway.

So I asked Albert if he could get me a deal and, since he was renegotiating Peter, Paul and Mary's contract with Warner Bros., he made their signing me part of the deal.

And, as Paul Simon prophesied, I was suddenly an artist.

TRACK 44 – SELF-COMPOSED

There's something that begs to be addressed at this point. Although being a writer has always been most important to me, whatever "creds" I have are a result of whatever-it-is-I-do with the work of <u>other</u> writers. As a producer, not a writer.

Consequently if you were intrigued enough to pick up this book, chances are 98.46 out of 100 (another made-up statistic) that you never knew I made any albums of my own.

Well, now you know.

So Albert got me a record deal. And I was eager to get started on this album of my own.

There seems to have always been a laziness among those record company execs who hired producers to just copy success, to look at the charts and hire the producers who were currently the most successful. In 1969, as a producer with some hits, I was busy. So, all of a sudden I was a record-producer-in-demand.

And, because I was busy, my album project would have to be done bit-by-bit, whenever I could squeeze in a session.

With the first break in my producing schedule, I jumped right into it. Of course I booked the studio I was most comfortable in: Columbia's Studio A on the penthouse floor of 799 Seventh Avenue.

I got Harvey Brooks to play bass. And young guitarist John Hall who had just played on the Seals and Crofts album for me. And

John's friend, drummer Wells Kelly and Harvey's friend, Paul Harris on organ. It was a two-keyboard-one-guitar rhythm section, a very familiar set up for me.

I was flying solo. There was no other producer. As for a recording budget, I was so used to working with big, profitable artists that I paid no attention to the costs. All the bills were just sent to Warners.

As with almost all First Albums, I already had written a bunch of the songs. So I had a head start. I'd write the rest of the songs as I went. Some of the songs came from personal experience but some were inspired by outside influences.

For instance, the inspiration for "Motorcycle Man" came from the movie, "The Wild One" with Marlon Brando and Lee Marvin. I got Rick Danko and Richard Manuel to play on that song with me. I was so happy to have Richard 's bumpy-galumphy drumming, a blur of flying elbows and drumsticks—and, as I've said earlier, "bumpy-galumphy" is a complimentary adjective.

Bob Dylan later told me he liked "Motorcycle Man". Wow.

Robbie Robertson had suggested I use an up-and-coming guitar player named Duane Allman. Duane and I got together for a session in New York City and recorded some songs that didn't make the final cut.

Duane suggested I go to Muscle Shoals to record.

Muscle Shoals was a trip! Like Haight-Ashbury, it was another world I'd never visited before.
Brooke and I checked into the Boll Weevil Cornpone Motel and, reeling from culture shock, she wanted a drink – quick.
But Muscle Shoals, Alabama was dry: no liquor sales.

The desk clerk was familiar with this conundrum. He made a phone call and told us to wait in a booth in the coffee shop.

In a while the sheriff arrived. "Y'all named Simon?" he asked.

Uh-oh, were we about to get busted for just <u>asking</u> about alcohol? He settled his bulk across from us and closed a curtain that discretely separated us from the rest of the restaurant. "What'd y'all want? I got bourbon and gin."

Legality, morality, sobriety. It's a local thing.

I had to put the project on the shelf for quite a while when a producing job took me to California.

Hearing that I was in town, Joe Smith, the V.P. of Warners called me into his office and said, "You've spent $64,000. Where's the record?"

So I resolved to finish up.

I had an idea for a song to go on the album attributing the inspiration for my writing as coming from some sort of Universal Inspiration Bank that we can all draw from.

But, as a stand-in for that lofty notion, I took Divine Inspiration down a couple of notches and chalked it all up to elves.

Once upon a time
In the Land of Rhyme,
There was a ship at sail upon a magic sea
And stowed away on board was me.
On the galley shelves
Was food for elves
And the elves rowed along singing this song
For anyone who happened to be along and for themselves.

JOHN SIMON

So, in the song, I pictured myself aboard a ship that I suspected contained some of that Universal Inspiration I was looking for. But I couldn't hear the words the elves were singing.
Later in the song, I got close enough to listen

> *You can make it out if you listen clear.*
> *It's nothing you wouldn't want to hear.*
> *They're singing, "Folderol"*
> *And something about elves being tall.*
> *And they're singing "Holy, holy, holy."*
> *Cuz these elves believe in God*
> *And the possibility of dying in the fog*
> *And fortunes on the run*
> *And the power of a gun,*
> *Battles lost and battle won*
> *And staying clear until they're done,*
> *Having kids and having fun*
> *And sailing high across the sun*
> *Till out of rhymes they've run ...*

(1969)

So, a-hah! They were following that advice given to beginning writers everywhere: "Write about what you know". In their case, Elf Experiences!

After we cut the track I asked Leon Russell, who had played on the track, to hang around and sit in the producer's chair while I overdubbed a vocal intro.
So I let loose with some unfettered scat-singing and, after the eight bar intro, Leon said, "Wow! But we weren't ready for that. Do it again."

I said "sure", but take 2 (the take on the record) wasn't as wild as the take they weren't ready for. I was a jazz-head in free-improvisation mode and, when you're improvising, you can't step in the same water twice.

***

Album # 2, "Journey":

When I first broke into the business in the early Sixties, recording contracts generally assumed an artist would deliver one album every year. Today's artists have more control over their product and release albums whenever they want to. But Warner Brothers asked me for a second album of my own a year after the first one was released. So I started putting that album together.

I felt bad about spending almost $70,000 on the first album, especially since it didn't recoup its investment for Warner Brothers, so I resolved to do this second one on the cheap. Instead of stretching the recording over several months and adding colors in overdub sessions, I decided to record it all live in 3 days – and that I did.

Peter Shane compared my first album to this one in the Harvard Crimson:

> "*The styles of the two albums differ dramatically. The first offers a tight weave of sentiment and fantasy, a mixture of songs falling in the folk-blues realm ... "Journey" is no less unusual for its verbal or musical qualities, but all the more exciting for its greater freedom in execution. The style ranges from honky-tonk, to Gershwinian melancholy, to high-energy, upbeat popular jazz, to barroom bluesiness more reminiscent of Simon's earlier songs.*"

Because of the difference in the 2 albums, the first carefully labored and rock-ish, this one free-swinging and spontaneous, each has a distinct set of enthusiasts who just "don't get" the other album. Interesting.

I love this album.

***

"Crazyfans"

It took 20 years for me to make another album. In 1991, my pal, George James, working at Bearsville Studios at the time, told me that a couple of Japanese gentlemen were nosing around Woodstock asking if I was still alive. I was glad to report that I was.

They were looking for me because the 2 albums that I'd recorded for Warners in 1970 and 1972 had just been released on CD in Japan and I had acquired "crazyfans" because of them.

> The electronics company, Pioneer was starting a record label.
> I would be their first release, Pioneer 001.

Sitting in a cab with Hiro Asano of Pioneer, I asked him how big the budget was and in his discreet, Japanese way he wrote a number on a slip of paper and handed it to me. Was I dreaming?! This was a budget comparable to the "good old days" before there even WERE budgets, when you just spent whatever it took to make an album.
So I was able to hire the best musicians I knew: Cornelius Bumpus, Ron Carter, Grady Tate, Terry Silverlight, Paul Ramsey, Toots Thielmans, The Brecker Brothers, Lew Soloff, George Young, Garth Hudson, Levon Helm, Rick Danko, John Sebastian, John Hall…
George James co-produced it with me in a top recording studio.
Yippee!

> When I did my first two solo albums I paid no attention at all to the quality of my voice. But for some reason, by 1991, I started to care. So my singing now was different. I mostly tried to sing in tune.
> Rick Danko coached me by telling me to "note it" when I practiced.
> What he meant was to leave out the consonants in the lyrics and just sing the vowels, which are the only real "notes".
> And C.C. urged me to push more air through my vocal chords.
> Both of these tips were very helpful.

When this new record came out I was not at all embarrassed by my singing but I heard from some fans of my earlier records that they <u>preferred</u> my original out-of-tune vocals.

There's no pleasing everyone.

Some songs take years to come together. Some are never finished; I have some I've been tinkering with for 50 years!
But rarely does a song materialize almost instantaneously out of the ether (where songs live before their discovered).

One of them did and came about this way:

Rolling Stone Magazine ran one of it's self-ascribed "definitive" lists of the best rock records EVER and I noticed that there were no Beach Boys songs, no Beatles, no Lovin' Spoonful, no Young Rascals ... nothing positive. They were all songs of teenage despair and angst. To Rolling Stone, it appeared, rock and roll was an open wound.

So there was my song title. And the lyrics rolled out in just a few minutes.

Rock and Roll is an Open Wound
It is finally feeling free and then marooned.
It's kids in their rooms smashin' the wall
Feelin' so bad or scared that they can't feel at all.

Rock and roll is kids on the street.
Gotta get outta the house and meet
Searchin' for truth in the dark A.M,
You only can trust your friends and sometimes not them.

It's the hurt of a love lost.
It is friendship crossed.

It's a heart harpooned.
Rock and Roll is an Open Wound.

Rock and roll is the beat of a drum.
It's a primitive kind of explosion that makes you all numb.
It's the joy of release, a scream from within
It's the fight of original grace with original sin.

Jazz is the urge to fly
And classical music is a chin held high.
The Blues is a howl at the moon
But Rock and Roll is an Open Wound.

It's the hurt of a love lost.
It is friendship crossed.
It's tryin' to keep that guitar tuned.
Rock and Roll is an Open Wound.

(1991)

So I recorded it for my new Japanese album, with help from Garth Hudson and John Hall, and that was that.

Then a couple of years later, I received this email (excerpted):

Dear John

I am not very music savvy, but I ran into this recording in a music store in Portland, Oregon and bought it for the above song.

I work in a maximum security institution which houses young men from 15 to 25 yrs. of age. I am the alcohol and drug treatment coordinator and co-facilitate a violent offender program. I play your song for my treatment groups to help them recognize what has happened in their lives and how to identify their feelings. They have had incredible responses to the words. They cry … They become angry … But after debriefing what they are feeling after listening to the words, they are willing to talk about their difficult years, feelings that no one ever really understood.

I have been grateful for this song for a long time and never knew how to tell you what you have done for a huge number of young angry men who are looking for answers. They begin to understand why they pass those feelings on to their victims.

I guess what I would really like to say to you is THANK YOU FOR THE WORDS AND THE UNDERSTANDING OF YOUNG PEOPLE WHO WANT AN UNDERSTANDING OF WHO THEY ARE AND WHY THEY FEEL THE WAY THEY DO! (caps original)

Hope your world is giving back to you and your efforts to put feelings into words.

Tanya Snider

Well, whether or not the world gave back to me, this letter certainly did. It's one of the best I've ever received. To know that a song that was cast out into the great void had some positive effect moves me more than I could have ever imagined it would.

I called the album "Out On The Street", the title of a song I wrote for Levon to sing over the credits of a TV special about homelessness.

George and I went to a piano factory in Queens and convinced them to roll a grand out onto the sidewalk for the cover photo.

And then, in 1992, thanks to Yoshi Nagato, my "man-in-Japan", I was invited to bring a band to Tokyo to play at The Blue Note jazz club.

CC would come along as a singer and percussionist and we both were so excited we literally started jumping up and down about this trip to the other side of the world. "We're going to Japan! We're going to Japan!"

Over the years I've been invited back for several other tours of Japan. The first time we were real excited. But, after the 4th or 5th trip, it was, "Going to Japan? Oh, no."
15 hours on a plane and jet lag somewhere on the scale between Rip Van Winkle and Snow White.

***

"HARMONY FARM"

Recorded in 1995, this may be my favorite of my own albums. For one thing I got to record it on my own piano.

I'll bet you never gave it a thought that piano players are at the mercy of the instrument they encounter in a studio, a concert hall or a club. Unless we're happy to play electric pianos (I don't love them.), we don't carry our ax around with us (the exception being superstars, particularly classical artists, whose piano may accompany them from gig to gig on the road).

So you never know what beauty or beast you may find. There are tales of piano players, particularly back in the days of the traveling Big Bands, who would take a sledge hammer to a particular instrument after struggling through a gig with it, or set it on fire.

> One year when I was touring with a Princeton Triangle show some of the pianos I ran into were real monsters whose jagged broken keys were the monster's teeth. One number in the show required a Jerry Lee Lewis sort of gliss, whipping the back of my hand up and down the keyboard and I'd end the night with blood on the keys.
>
> But Stan Szelest who played with The Reconstituted Band taught me something. He would keep a empty soft cigarette pack lying at the end of the keyboard. Whenever he needed to play a gliss like that, he avoided the bloody keys result by slipping his hand inside the empty pack and slathering it up and down the keys.

> > "Every piano's different in its special way
> > You never can tell until you sit down and play
> > Some play easy and some play rough
> > Either way. You know, I can't get enough.
> > Just like a monkey starin' at a banana,
> > That's me, when I see a piana."
> >
> > (Piano-Playing Fool, 1995)

I bought my own piano way back in 1967 from a guy who dealt in pianos. I was looking for a Steinway (doesn't everybody?) but the minute I played this particular Mason & Hamlin, I fell in love with the rich bass notes and the ease of playing it. It has moved with me 5 times and has been shot.

Want to read that again? I'll wait ...

Yes, it was shot. I had a humidifying unit under the piano and, when its tank needed to be filled with water, a red light installed on the piano would blink.

> One night when the house was empty, a half-mad 22-year old broke in and, seeing the blinking light, aimed the shotgun he happened to be carrying at the light and blew a 3" hole in the side of the piano.
> This is one of the features of living in the country: some people don't feel dressed without their shotgun.

***

"HOME"
In 1998, Pioneer coaxed a third album out of me.

> With the exception of Fran Landesman's lyrics to "Poems To Eat" on my "Journey" album, I'd never included a song whose words were completely written by someone else.
> That changed when I recorded a beautiful poem by the Japanese rock star, Moto Sano. Moto writing in a language that was not his own, revealed great insight into human nature. His poem was called "Love Planets". The stanzas end as follows:

I: *You are always right.*
   I am always wrong.

II: *I am always right.*
    You are always wrong.
III: *One of us is right.*
    One of us is wrong.
And, finally,
IV: *Both of us are right*
    Both of us are wrong."

(Love Planets, Motoharu Sano, 1996)

* * *

Greatest Hits

In 2000, Pioneer Records requested a Greatest Hits compilation of songs from the albums I'd done for them. They called it "THE BEST AND BEYOND" and they let me select my favorites.

It happened that Rick Danko had just died.

His widow, Elizabeth said that Rick had kept an appreciative "certificate" I had made for him in 1986 framed on his wall.

I wanted to include something in his honor and I felt moved to sing "Sometimes I Feel Like A Motherless Child".

* * *

<u>"NO BAND".</u>

In an earlier version of this very book you are reading I had appended an appendix containing some of my favorite songs I'd written.

But my friend, John Sebastian, pointed out, "Those're only the lyrics. What's the use if you can't hear the songs?"

He was right about that.

I think I've said earlier that I don't consider myself much of a singer. I always wished others would sing my songs. Well, in hopes of that, in 2005 I decided to record an album of just me singing them, demo-style, with a piano.

There are some of my older songs on there, like "Two Ways Of Lookin' At The Same Thing", "Motocycle Man" and "Lost" and some that had never seen the light of day before like "Time Stands Still In The Shower" (from my "Archie and Veronica" musical), "Irresistible" and the politically-piqued "Why Do The Bad Guys Do What They Do".

And that's it. Those are the albums of my own stuff that have been released.

Thank you for your attention.

TRACK 45 – NIHONGO

Yoshi Nagato booked several more tours of Japan after that first gig at The Blue Note in Tokyo and then I got some calls to produce Japanese artists. The cross-cultural experience of working with them was enlightening and often amusing for us all.

<u>Toku</u>, a young jazz vocalist and flugelhorn player, came to NYC to record.

He accorded the highest honor and deference to the jazz greats in the band that I assembled for him, which was quite different from my attitude: in my mind we were all equals, each of us just one-of-the-guys-in-the-band.

One of the charts was very difficult and drummer Grady Tate was asking me questions about the music in front of him when I said, "No. No. Just hold on, Grady. We'll run it down and then it'll be clear."

Toku came rushing into the control room and said to me, "Never, never say 'no' to Mister Grady Tate!!"

Ah, well.

Then there was Moto Sano, whose popularity in Japan was equivalent to Bruce Springsteen's here.
He came to Woodstock with his entourage to record because he wanted to supplement his Japanese band of excellent hand-picked players with Woodstock musicians instead of the NYC talent pool.

His players were in awe of the Woodstock musicians who would drop by the studio. When Moto's drummer extended his hand in greeting to Levon, he introduced himself: "Yutah!"
Levon replied, "Arkansas!"

Later that year, Moto invited Garth and me to Japan to play as guests in this HUGE concert he was giving in Osaka. Garth brought a mysterious suitcase with him that he allowed no one else to handle. I imagined it contained an exotic and fragile musical instrument.

The night of the show, several pert uniformed young women showed up to help us from the hotel to the coliseum next door and, when they attempted to carry the mysterious suitcase, there was a struggle as Garth insisted on carrying it himself.

When we got to the dressing room and he opened it the mystery was solved. It contained Garth's precious performance hat with its hatband of Crocodile Dundee alligator teeth.

TRACK 46 – PHILIPPE & TWYLA

You can spot most recording engineers and active record producers and studio musicians because they have "studio pallor". Those late hours in climate-controlled environments. Sometimes they look like The Walking Dead.

For that reason and several others, I've seldom turned down a chance to leave the studios and walk through fresh fields.
For instance, there was the opportunity to write some circus music.

I met Philippe Petit a short while after he walked between the World Trade Towers.
Jim Signorelli, a talented close friend who for years directed all the commercial parodies for Saturday Night Live, introduced us and Philippe asked me to write some music for his stint with The Big Apple Circus which was a lot of fun to do, writing for a circus band. I used Stravinsky's "Histoire Du Soldat" as my model for the small orchestra.

And in 1979 came a chance to write ballet music, when Robbie Robertson recommended me to Twyla Tharp.

Twyla is a gifted iconoclast of a choreographer. I am no connoisseur of The Dance but her reputation in the Capezio set was considerable.
She needed music for the Finale of her show that year at BAM, The Brooklyn Academy Of Music.
The music would be pre-recorded.

She took a minimalist approach (She is also a musician). She wanted only one chord – 15 minutes of it!

Philippe   Twyla

And she also wanted that insistent bass drum of disco for 15 minutes. Roy Markowitz, the drummer for the recording, had calf muscles the size of cantaloupes by the time the song was over.

Then in1980, the year after we worked together for her BAM finale, it was Twyla's idea to create something bigger for Broadway: a musical in which dance would have a greater role than dialogue, a "dansical".

> The music I wrote for the BAM finale had been pre-recorded. But this time I would conduct the 20-piece orchestra live in the pit of the Winter Garden theater (where "Cats" would follow us and remain for years.) I felt an actual shiver run through me at the prospect of my music ringing through a theater where once upon a time my idols had heard theirs performed.

And I was facing the challenge that comes with all original, new music. Once I heard the score being played, there would be copying mistakes and little adjustments. But correcting those errors would require time and a hefty budget, neither of which we had.

We rehearsed the music at Carroll Studios on 41st Street and, in the room next door, an orchestra was rehearsing a revival of "Oklahoma"—reading music that had been played thousands of times before. The Oklahoma producers, with their hefty budget, had booked a week for their hardly necessary rehearsals. For our score, never played before and peppered with things that needed to be fixed, because of our smaller budget, we had just 2 days of rehearsals. Any further corrections would have to be made during the performance.

What to do?

I hit on the idea of "The Pit Parade". It was a nightly newspaper just for the orchestra. I conducted the performances with a baton in one hand and a red pencil in the other. And when I heard mistakes, I'd scribble a mark on the score in front of me, then go home and work on tomorrow's edition of The Pit Parade which would say things like, "Oboe, that's a B-flat in measure 214." "Strings are too loud in the fugue", etc.

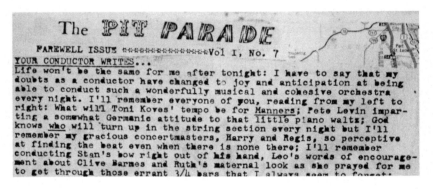

The guys in the orchestra got in on it too. Before long, there were "personals" in the paper.

"Wally has a Selmer bari with a low-A for sale. Reasonably priced." "Could Barry, move his crash cymbal farther from my head, please?" etc.

It was the most popular publication in the orchestra pit of the St. James Theater.

TRACK 47 — BROADWAY: "ROCK 'N ROLL"

My ambition during all this has always been to be a Broadway composer—like Frank Loesser, Cole Porter, Richard Rodgers, George Gershwin, Meredith Wilson ... the list of my idols went on and on.

So, while producing records, I generally had an unfinished project for a musical in progress on the side.

By 1983 Ed Kleban, who had been a low-level staff producer with me at Columbia, had had a major major major success in having written the lyrics to "A Chorus Line" and he urged me to join the BMI Musical Theater Workshop, where Lady Luck had tapped him on the shoulder and gotten him the "Chorus Line" assignment. I resisted because I didn't fancy the idea of going back to "school". But I joined up and thrived in the workshop.

The musical I worked on there based on the "Archie and Veronica" comics was almost produced. The comic book company that owned the rights sent a couple of musical "experts" to an audition I assembled and the experts gave the show their wholehearted approval. But for some reason, known only to the mentality of certain managers, my manager, Scott Shukat urged me to wait. Then, while I was waiting, Paramount, a Hollywood motion picture studio, bought the rights and continued to renew them each year – without ever coming up with a viable treatment.

That was extremely frustrating for me because I knew I had written a good show. So, to avoid the issue of rights, I followed that musical with one that was totally original which I called, "Billionaire Embryos".

> It was based on a true news story about some unborn in vitro fetuses that had become incredibly wealthy after their parents suddenly died after naming them sole heirs in their wills. It's a comedy. And the cast was small: four people. It seemed eminently do-able.

Maybe someday it'll be produced.

Meanwhile I had been involved in a few Broadway projects. In 1982 I was asked to be the Musical Supervisor of a show called "Rock and Roll: The First 5000 Years". It was the brainchild of Bob Gill and Bob Rabinowitz (collectively called "The Bobs"). They had been the creators of the extremely successful "Beatlemania" in which 4 mop-top actors recreated the music of The Beatles in front of video projections of The Sixties.

The Bobs's idea for this new show was to trace the entirety of Rock and Roll from its beginnings to the present, in front of projections of the entirety of history since the dawn of civilization.

Sort of a logical extension of their first show in some respects but, other than the logic of it, the concept was a little far-fetched and cumbersome.

The producer was the gifted and even-tempered Jules Fisher, a renowned lighting designer, and the director was the brilliant Joe Layton, who had won multiple Emmy and Tony awards and worked with stars as different as Barbra Streisand and Richard Pryor.

Jules   Joe

Instead of the 4 actors of "Beatlemania", we had about 20 and they were so fine. They were such dead-on imitators of the artists we were replicating. Some of them could imitate 5 or 6 different singers perfectly. I called them "human jukeboxes".

In fact Madonna auditioned for the show and we wanted her but she told us that she intended instead to go to Hollywood and cut a demo. I wonder whatever became of her ...

The world of Broadway is full of wild anecdotes and rumors, as you'd imagine. One that was going around at the time and alleged to be true (though I have to classify it here as Hearsay) was this one:

Although Musical Theater owed a debt to the English Music Hall tradition (as well as to vaudeville, on this side of The Pond), the genre had thrived in America without much international intervention. That changed. Around the same time as The British Invasion of rock and roll, the Brits invaded American Musical Theater and leading the charge, mounted on the twin steeds of "Cats" and "The Phantom Of The Opera", was their composer, Andrew Lloyd Weber.

Andrew was not a favorite of the Old Hands of Broadway apparently. So when he asked Alan Jay Lerner, the lyricist of "My Fair Lady". "Camelot", "Gigi" and "Brigadoon", why people seemed to take an instant dislike to him, Lerner replied, "Probably to save time."

Cruel, but funny.

TRACK 48 – TV:
"THE COMEDY ZONE"

In 1984, I was approached to be the Musical Director of a TV variety show, the job description filled in the past by a number of luminaries: Skitch Henderson, Doc Severinsen, Paul Shaffer, Branford Marsalis, Jon Baptiste, et al.

This was to be a CBS summer replacement show called "The Comedy Zone". The concept was to bring in Broadway writers and actors. So among the writers were Wendy Wasserstein, Christopher Durang, John Patrick Shanley and John Bishop and in the cast were Mark Linn Baker, Joe Mantegna, Judd Hirsch, Kathleen Turner and a bunch of other fine actors. The director was the skillful stage director Gerry Guiterrez.

> I was thrilled to meet Venerable Entertainer Steve Allen who was slated to be the host. We had production meetings and he was constantly coming up with one-liners like "I want to thank you from the bottom of my mouth."

I'd never done TV before. It was all done live-to-tape before an audience. Then in post-production it was edited and "reinforced" with additional applause.

In other words, a laugh track.

And that actually was a huge eye-opener that confirmed my observations about how dumb most TV sitcoms were.

I went out to Hollywood for editing sessions.

Picture this:

We were there waiting for the Laugh Track Guy to show up. Then he peeled into the studio parking lot in his pickup with a contraption in the back that looked like one of those bulky old battery-chargers that every lonesome gas station in the Fifties used to have in the back of their greasy garage.

That was the Laugh Track machine.

On the machine were several volume controls, each connected to a tape loop of laughing people ranging from a few solitary nervous giggles to a huge crowd pissing in their pants from The Funniest Thing They Had Ever Heard.

So we sat in this control room playing the video of the show and the Laugh Track Guy was reacting and pushing up the faders according to <u>what struck HIM as funny</u>.

Now the problem was, as you can imagine, everything depended on that guy's sense of humor. And that particular Laugh Track Guy was more a fan of The Three Stooges than he was of, say, George Carlin. So when a line that we thought was real funny came up, sometimes he didn't respond at all.

"Buddy, what about that joke?" we asked.

"Uh, I don't get it."

But if one actor gave another actor a dirty look in a scene, the artificial audience would burst out as if their naked skin had been tickled by 1000 feathers.

And that explains a lot of TV sitcoms that we've all seen.

TRACK 49 – HOLLYWOOD: WILSON PICKETT, HITLER AND DONALD DUCK.

There is a degree of cross pollination in the arts, so it's no surprise that my career as a record producer might spill into the world of "pictures", as Hollywood insiders used to refer to their trade.

My first involvement in a movie was when I was approached, after a little success, to write the music for the movie, "Last Summer".
I wrote a few songs for it (there is a recorded album of the music) and some underscoring. The people that hired me, United Artists, encouraged me to get some star singers on board.

The first star I approached was Wilson Pickett to sing a song I wrote for him called "Lay Your Love On Me".
I met him at Atlantic Records. He showed up, in the hottest day in August, in a full-length black mink coat that was the twin of the one Clive Davis wore backstage at The Fillmore East. I played the song for him. He liked it and said he'd do it.
When asked what his fee would be, he said $20,000 for that one song. Since the total budget for the film music was $20,000, I had the option of having one song sung a capella by Wilson Pickett or having several performers sing several songs.

Though it would have been pretty far out to just have Wilson Pickett singing one song unaccompanied for the entire length of the picture, it seemed a little avant-garde and impractical.

There are 2 more Hollywood stories that would've changed my life but didn't:

> In 1985, the unproduced musical I'd written based on the "Archie" comics drew the attention of some executives at Disney. (Disney! The home of Mickey Mouse and Donald Duck. That's something!)
> They flew me out to Hollywood to talk about writing a movie based on "The Nutcracker" and their appreciation of my songs and their enthusiasm and encouragement were so great that I flew back to New York eager to get to work.
>
> They said they'd be in touch.
>
> I never heard from them again.
>
> It's the old joke:
> How do they say "fuck you" in Hollywood?
> Answer: "I love your work."

And around that same time (the actual year has blurred for me at this point) I came really close to a crucial change of locale and life.
Mo Ostin, the president of Warner Bros. Records, flew C.C. and me out to California to discuss the possibility of my becoming the Music Director of Warner pictures.
I felt I had some inside information about this job opportunity because I knew the current Music Director, Larry Marks who had previously worked at Columbia.

So Mo invited us to dinner at his house. The three of us sat at a table that could have comfortably seated the entire cast of "Gone with the Wind" while his cook served us a dinner that I recall featured frozen peas and Mo told us how great our life would be out there, how C.C. would get lots of work acting and how, as the Music Director of Warner pictures, I could eventually ease myself into conducting the orchestra at the Oscar awards.

Sounded pretty exciting.

> So the next day, a Friday as I recall, I went in to spend the day
> with Larry in his Music Director office.
> It was easy. Basically Larry and his two secretaries hung around
> doing nothing all day which, to me, seemed like it would afford
> me plenty of time to write music or anything that came into my
> head.
>
> But then at 5 o'clock on that Friday afternoon, Larry's phone
> rang and I saw him jump to attention the same way my first boss,
> Charlie Burr would snap out of a reverie when a call came in
> from Goddard Lieberson.
>
> It turned out that Warners had released a concert movie by Led
> Zeppelin and, as Warners' Music Director, Larry was the contact
> man at the movie company. The man on the other end of the
> phone was Led Zeppelin's manager.
> He was calling because the band was playing a big concert some-
> where in Texas and guitarist Jimmy Page, for some perverse
> reason, was going to appear in a full Hitler costume and the
> manager wanted to do him one better by surprising him wearing
> a Mussolini outfit.
> He was calling Larry because he needed size 14 Mussolini boots
> and it was now Larry's job to try to round up a pair and get them
> to Dallas at 5 o'clock on a Friday afternoon.

Was this how I envisioned my future life?

Uh-uh. I decided to return to the bootless world of New York where
any number of possibilities might come up. But it was unlikely that they
would involve costuming.

TRACK 50 – COLLABORATION

So C.C. and I moved back East and work slowed down for me.

But that was O.K. Popular music was changing too. The stuff I enjoyed working with was losing popularity to Disco and Heavy Metal, the former cocaine-based and the latter smelling of alcohol.

Then, in 1981, with the arrival of MTV and the music video, the whole nature of popular music changed more radically than most people even noticed.

It might be hard for a young person now to realize how popular music used to be experienced.

The main difference of course was that it was a "blind" experience. You mostly listened to music, you didn't see it.

Little by little after 1981 fans of pop music were led to take it for granted that a song would be both aural AND visual. And it seemed an artist was being evaluated as much by how he or she or they <u>looked</u> as to how they sounded.

Music was no longer a "blind medium".

Music video <u>directors</u> assumed the importance that record <u>producers</u> had once enjoyed.
I was just as happy to ease on out of the hurly-burly of pop music and settle into our house in the country and the somewhat laid-back rural life that made C.C. and me real happy.

But there wasn't any grass growing under our feet. No pun intended.

First I put together a Johnny Mercer show that ran at The Bottom Line in NY and wrote music for an N.P.R. radio news magazine, wrote a bunch of "serious" music and gigged around.

And, now that her kids were school-age and no longer needed constant mothering, C.C. got back into showbiz.

Let me amplify that statement.

C.C. was raised in Las Vegas. Growing up, she must've seen every act, every comic who played in the Vegas showrooms and lounges.

At an early age she was infected by the ShowBiz Bug. She had a radio show called "Teen Time With Caroline."

Living in that wild and wooly town, she collected a passel of stories.

Like, when she was 13, she met Elvis.

Her mother owned a bar, appropriately named "Mother's Bar", whose silent partner was the sheriff. When he heard that C.C. was nuts about Elvis, he arranged for her to meet him in his suite in the El Rancho Vegas. Ushered by the sheriff through the sea of damp and screaming teens outside the hotel, she was whisked up to his suite and, as she describes it, "There he was, wearing a powder blue jumpsuit and blue suede shoes, smoking a cigar and holding a drink – which was a shock cuz everyone knew that Elvis neither smoked nor drank."

Now, twenty years later, her first forays back into the world of showbiz were as a mime. She was one of 4 live actors on a Sesame Street sort of show for the debut season of the Nickelodeon channel called "Pinwheel House".

The former Coco, The Mime still gets fan mail, the strangest of which came from a man who remembered that he had insisted that his governess dress as Coco before tucking him in at night.

After that, the mime wanted to talk so she started to work as an actor with a voice and soon become a Lifetime Member of the prestigious Actors Studio.

She collected a lot of her Vegas tales and put together a one-woman caba-ret show, "No One Comes From Vegas."

Then, when she was booked into the Byrdcliffe Theater in Woodstock, she needed an opening act at the last minute and so I happily rushed in on my white steed to fill the void.

And from that point on, she and I became Creative Collaborators.

Shortly we were performing as a duo with a show called "Alone Together For The First Time Again". We went out on the road. We played some cabarets in NYC and venues in the East, the South (St. Pete, Florida) and West (Hollywood). We wrote our own stuff. It was Big Fun.

At some point in the early Nineties, at the urging of Susan Batson, her act-ing mentor and later Coach-To-The-Stars, she developed a semi-factual full-length play centering around her family going to watch the A-bomb tests in the desert when she was about nine years old.
The play was eventually named "Jackass Flats", the Vegas locals' name for the A-bomb test site.

Over time I got more involved in the writing of the play and we worked on it at The Actors Studio where we got some very helpful help from qualified theater pros, like Arthur Penn, the director of "Bonnie and Clyde" and Bill Goldman who wrote "Butch Cassidy and The Sundance Kid."

Along the way, our play won an award for the Best Unproduced Play of 1995

> Then, almost 20 years after we started writing the piece, it had its official professional Actors Equity full production, a premiere at the Shadowland Theater in Ellenville NY, directed by the talented Brendan Burke.

> And then, the next summer, we had a short run as part of The Fringe Festival in NYC. As fate would have it, our daughter, Sienna, by now a trained actor herself, played the role based on her own grandmother in the Fringe production.

Our friend, political cartoonist Bob Grossman, drew our poster:

The careful reader might note that C.C. is not her given name.

Her name change came about this way:

It was The Sixties and a lot of "enlightened" folks were crossing our path, many genuine, many bogus. One who might be suspected of falling into the latter category, who called himself a "psychic", told Caroline that to ensure professional success her last name should begin with the letter "L".

Always intrigued by playing games, we went on the search for "L" last names: Lassiter, Leary, Lawson, Logan, Lewis, Lincoln, LaRue, Lickelbacher, Lindbergh, Lebowski, Lunchmeat, …

Then Sienna, six years old at the time, , said, "Mom, how about 'Loveheart'?"

And that was it.

So, initializing her given name, she became C.C. Loveheart.

When we first started working together, she wrote one of the most poignant stanzas I've come across:

If to say "I love you"
Means I cannot love all others
Then how can I love you
Except from a small, dark corner of my heart?

TRACK 51 – HOW TO MAKE A RECORD

When I started out at Columbia. I might have been asked at a typical NYC cocktail party the inevitable NYC cocktail party question, "What do you do? And I'd answer, "I'm a record producer".

Then their inevitable follow-up would be, "What's a record producer?"

> Trying to keep things understandable, I would say that a record producer does for a record what both a director and producer do for a movie – except for raising the money.

That was a simple answer that worked then. But that didn't cover it. Soon I rephrased the answer to that question.

> My answer to "What is a record producer?" became … ANYBODY.

And anyone back then could have been a producer. An engineer, an arranger, a manager, a friend, a fan. We were as different as our backgrounds had made us.

> These days, with the proliferation of inexpensive high-level home recording equipment, the answer "Anybody" is even more true. And that goes for recording in your bedroom or your garage.

Maybe the only thing that successful producers have in common, whether the recording takes in a professional studio or in a garage is that we're all psychologists. It takes a lot for an artist to make a record. He or she is laying his or her art out there on the line and the nerves and the stress of doing that can be considerable. So a producer has to be skillful in the psychology of bringing the project to completion.

(I just figured that out last week.)

That might be a funny thing to say but there's Truth in it too. At first I was slow to consider people's feelings. I covered up my youth and inexperience with a certain wise-ass arrogance and self-importance and I now regret any hurt that I caused with that attitude.
More recently I worked with a Broadway conductor who wore a T-shirt that said, "Except for the lead dog, the view is the same." I thought, "How pompous of him." But there was a time when that could've been me.

In the interest of those who might be interested, here are some of the things I've learned in a recording studio.

As far as the producer's hands-on involvement in the actual recording process, it all depends on the artist.

Paul Simon and Art Garfunkel, for example, kept their boat pointed in the direction of "Finished Record Land". So it was my job to put together recording sessions that aimed for the things they imagined and to make suggestions to which they could say "aye" or "nay".

On the other hand Michael Franks said he would write the songs and we'd pick the musicians together, but he left all the arrangements and everything else to me. Bless him!

And, on an even other hand, Den Dinkwad and The Genetic Mutations looked cute but that was it. They were light on talent and it was up to me to teach them how to play their instruments, how to sing, how to write songs and even, in the case of one obscure band, how to dice garlic.

(Note: don't bother searching for records
by Den Dinkwad. I made him up!)

COMMITMENT:

One thing I learned in my work with The Band was to COMMIT to a sound – committing to a certain kind of echo or tone quality or attitude, thereby LOCKING IN THE CONCEPT.

That way all the elements that follow would be aligned with that concept, and we wouldn't be wasting time or money on ideas that didn't fit with the overall purpose.

This is particularly apparent if there are overdubs.

For instance, one musician overdubbing may have something in mind, often his own part predominating.

Then another player, overdubbing later, may imagine that HIS part will predominate.

Then, when it comes time to mix, whose version of that Grand Notion are you going to aim for?

It's much better, as I see it, to settle on the concept early and have everyone adapt their playing to fit that idea.

MIXING:

If they haven't committed to a Grand Notion for a song, many producers and engineers will leave the elements of a recording as bare and dry as possible, each on a separate track (like each drum microphone) so that there's the option later of treating them in any number of ways and the mixing process ascends in importance.

There's the phrase, "We'll fix it when we mix it"—so common that it appeared on T-shirts seen in the studios.

Recording studios love that because it results in more billable studio time.

Also, when anyone first gets their hands on the controls to set the levels of all the elements in a mix, EVERYONE makes the same initial mistake (I did too), and this goes for mixing recorded music or for mixing a live performance.

We ask ourselves, "What do I want to hear more of?"

And before we know it, the controls for each instrument are pushed up to the maximum and there's no more room to raise up the musical elements we want to hear louder.

But instead why not ask, "What's too loud?"

And, shazam! New worlds open up. Budding engineers, if you can take one helpful thing from this book, that'd be it.

LISTENING BACK IN A RECORDING STUDIO:
Here's what it's like: it's great. The experience is pure and stripped-down. There are no distractions and noises from concert crowds or from the body language of performers. The focus is entirely on the music. The music is played back loud, the lights are low. The listener's eyes may be closed.

And the sound is so clear – you can hear EVERYTHING – which is often a drawback. Innumerable times I have had to urge artists not to fret over that one misplayed note or detail. In the course of a complete performance, the mistake will never be noticed. Even the temporarily dissatisfied artist will have forgotten about it the next day.

But the important thing in the studio doesn't lie in the details: it's the gestalt, the overall effect, the energy, the mood, the sincerity, the honesty of the performance. And, like others, I often have had to remind myself to consider the forest and overlook the trees.

Here's another thing that I found out that applies to all artists from Den Dinkwad to Pablo Casals – and surely applies to other disciplines in Life beyond making records:

> Each project begins with a vision – what you (the artist, the producer, the creative team) imagine the result of your labors will be. But then, at some point, particularly if you're getting frustrated because there seem to be roadblocks between you and your goal, it really makes sense to

- STOP
- FORGET THE DETAILS OF YOUR ORGINAL VISION
- LOOK INSTEAD AT WHAT YOU'VE ACTUALLY GOT
- BUILD ON THAT.

If you're lucky you'll find that either there's a new, unexpected route to your goal or a new and better goal has appeared.

It sure beats kicking a dead horse.

So making a record is a little like a board game. Start with the artist, go around the board, get to the record at the end. Game over.
Or you might say that you start with the idea of making a record and finally arrive at the record itself.

HOW TO MAKE A RECORD:

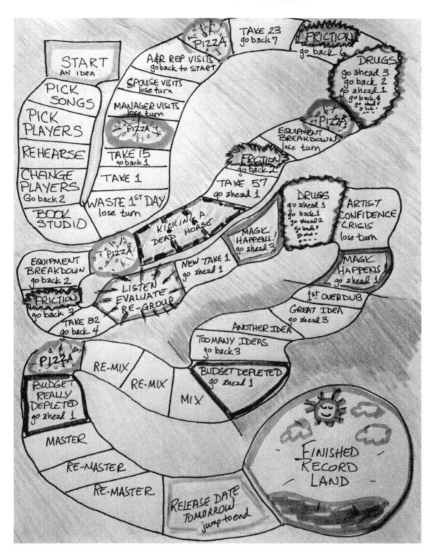

TRACK 52 – TECH'S SPECS

(**W**ARNING: for people like me who think that reading about audio engineering is about as boring as, well, reading about audio engineering, you can skim this Chapter/Track. Some people want to know about this stuff. Others might want to re-join the tour group for the next Track.)

Even though I've never cared to know the difference between an ohm and a volt, I figured I had to know at least a little something about audio engineering if making records was going to be my Day Job. I mean, just basic stuff – like if I were a shoe salesman I'd want to know which end of the shoe was the heel and which was the toe. Basic stuff.

Plus I actually found some of it historically interesting – like this:

THE BEGINNINGS.

Some of the earliest recordings were made at one time in one room with ingenious devices like railroad tracks to slide soft instruments toward the big recording horn when they were featured.

Also, the sharp stylus that cut the grooves in the recording cylinder had to move at a constant speed so the stylus was pulled by a cord tied to a weight that dropped at a steady rate. But the weight had to keep dropping until the recording was over so the musicians played on the top floor of a building and the weight fell through holes cut in the floors of the stories below.

OVER-DUBBING:

When I was growing up, some of my favorite records were by Les Paul and Mary Ford. They really had a different sound. Choruses of guitars and singers whose blend was so homogenized that they sounded like they had to be sisters. I thought this was the epitome of cool.

When I began to investigate as to how this was done I discovered that Les Paul was a tinkerer.

Since the beginning of recorded music, all the musicians had played at the same time in the same place. Then, around 1950, some Invention Bug got into Les's head.

He was the pioneer in overdubbing. He figured out that he could "ping-pong" back and forth between 2 tape machines, recording his guitar over and over again on top of each other until he achieved that thick texture all by himself. Then he did the same thing with the vocals of his wife, Mary.

And suddenly there was the sound of "Les and Mary" – or, more accurately, Lesses and Marys.

Les and Mary

(Actually, I wasn't far off when I said the vocals sounded like they had to be sisters. For their in-person shows, Mary's sister would sing the harmony parts from behind a curtain.)

RECORDING LIVE VERSUS OVER-DUBBING:
Les Paul's records came out in the 50's. So overdubbing, or layering or sweetening, is a comparatively recent development in music.

In the countless centuries prior to 1950, if as a composer you imagined more than one voice or instrument, you damn well had to get everyone together in the same place at the same time.

Don't get me wrong: As the records that I've made can attest, I LOVE the possibilities that overdubbing affords. But, every time I've had to put on headphones and overdub a part, on my own or someone else's record, I've found that it's really hard to emotionally throw myself back in time to the feeling in the room when the original tracks were laid down.

There is a precious, elusive <u>communal joy</u> in making music at the same time with others that is impossible to achieve when overdubbing.

> Something in the spontaneity, the mutual cooperation, the building of the common "vibe" gives a recording that elusive "magic" that so many aim for.
> Even so, it's a case of build-it-and-they-will-come. Once introduced, overdubbing was here to stay.

<u>STEREO</u>:
When I was growing up, the sound system in our home was decent because my dad liked to listen to his classical music, but the records in the home of a friend of mine sounded strikingly new and different. My dad's collection was, of course, monaural.

| 1877 | 1954 | 1957 |

Apparently the Invention Bug had camped out in the imaginations of some other engineers who posed this question: since we have 2 ears, shouldn't we have 2 speakers to accurately replicate what we hear?

And suddenly: stereo.

The first stereo record I heard had Dixieland music on one side of the album and sound effects on the other.

When I arrived at Columbia, stereo hadn't universally caught on yet. Singles at 45 RPM were monaural and, though the number of people who had bought a stereo rig was increasing, we still released 2 versions of every album, monaural and stereo. So we had to mix everything twice, everything twice.

THE PLOT SICKENS:

"Turning and turning in the widening gyre
The falcon cannot hear the falconer;
Things fall apart; the centre cannot hold;
Mere anarchy is loosed upon the world…"
("*The Second Coming*", William Butler Yeats, 1919)

I'm going to sound a little disgruntled at this point so brace yourself.

When pop music embraced Heavy Metal and Disco, I eased myself out of the studios for a while. But, during my absence, those Inventors of New Recording Equipment had not been sleeping. No Siree!

So when I went back in for a few projects, it seemed that anarchy had been loosed upon the recording studios.

Though there were still a lot of talented artists, musical talent was no longer a prerequisite. Engineers had designed ever more sophisticated machinery to compensate for the rough edges of performers, the most reprehensible, in my opinion, being the pitch-correcting machine.

And, in light of this book's title, the potential for "Lies" had blossomed.

If a singer had a hard time singing in tune, no problem. The singer's sketchy pitch-control could be processed so that notes became perfectly accurate, as if the vocalists had frets on their vocal chords.

That appalled me. I wouldn't do it. Thank Heaven I never had occasion to. If someone had worked hard to sing in tune and didn't require pitch-correcting assistance, I felt they were entitled to a reputation above and apart from those singers whose pitch needed to be artificially improved.

But then, I never used a "click track" either. A click track is essentially a metronome piped into the headphones of musicians to keep the beat steady while they're recording.

In the first place, that's the job of the drummer and the rhythm section. And, in the second place, music "breathes" to some degree: as the playing gets excited, the tempo speeds up a little. As it relaxes, it slows down.

That's natural, organic. A click track can't breathe.

But music capitalized on the mechanical nature of the click track, each beat precisely spaced from the last. Dancers could depend on that inevitable steadiness and disco music thrived.

Blasted loud, disco was Man-Submits-To-Machine.

Pitch-correcting. Click tracks.

Where others may have strived for a record with perfect, meticulously crafted technical elements, they hardly mattered to me compared to musical inspiration, natural talent, soul.

I'm always so happy to discover a relatively ancient recorded performance in which the artistry shines through the old scratchy noise. It's like an archeological dig.

Art versus technology.

Soul is not meticulous. Soul can have rough edges. Soul is human.

TRACK 53 — MISTAKEN IDENTITIES

"Hej! My old stranger, Rip!

"I am missing you. When do you come again to Svendenborg? We had large fun, yes?

"Are you getting my songs on top of the radio yet?

"You are probably losing my address so it's here. Please send me the 100 dollars you loaned from me.

"I always love you.

Birgita."

That's an approximation of an actual letter addressed to me c/o some record company. I kept it for a while but it's become lost in the dustbin of strange memorabilia. (Though it has had a lasting effect because some of my friends still call me "Rip".)

Of course it wasn't me.

One of the attractions of being a record producer for me was the anonymity of it. The Rock "personalities" I've worked with can't walk on the street, take a subway or partake of many of the joys of common life without being pestered or gawked at. (I know—I've been a gawker myself. If we really appreciated those celebs, we'd leave them alone. But we want to have some connection with those incandescent stars, from royalty to Rockers.)

I've kept a pretty low public profile. The only time I ever flaunted my legitimate connection with artists was to get past bouncers and get in free to clubs where they were performing.

But because of that anonymity, I've had imposters who've assumed the credentials of my producing career. That's flattering, I guess. But I feel bad when someone used my name to, for instance, borrow 100 bucks from some unsuspecting patsy in Scandanavia.

The letter from Birgita was just one consequence of my invisibility.

Another: my old friend, Harvey Brooks, was taking the Hertz shuttle to pick up his rental car at an airport when he struck up a conversation with the attractive shuttle driver. When, like any red-blooded American boy, he attempted to pick her up by telling her he was a credentialed rock and roll bass player, she said, "Oh, my husband is a record producer."

> You guessed it: she was married to Another Me. Someone who had pilfered my name and my credentials.
> I wonder how long that relationship lasted.

And there was a phone call from a young fellow in Washington, DC who asked if I knew him. I said his name wasn't familiar. He asked me if I was 5 foot 3, weighed 275 pounds and smoked Gitanes (I've forgotten the actual specs. Those are made up.).

He told me that Yet Another Me had signed his band to a production deal but he became suspicious when he visited Yet Another Me and discovered a room mysteriously full of phone books from cities all across the US.

> (For those under 40, "phone books" are what we used before the Internet.).

Imposters.

But I can assure you that an imposter is not writing this book.

Are you sure?

Of course there are bona fide John Simon musicians whose parents were as conventional as mine in assigning them first names. A jazz saxophonist. A guy in Ithaca who plays for kids' birthday parties. A guy in Oregon, one in New Orleans, another in Northern California. What is this, a sequel to "Invasion Of The Bodysnatchers"?

And there's a bulky NFL lineman. And there's the drama critic.

Maybe I should have changed my name to "Rip". But by that time it was a little late.

* * *

And here's a case of a theft not of a personal name but of a job title:

A&R.

A&R stands for Artists and Repertoire. But, at first, it was synonymous with Record Producer—one and the same job.

Those were the days when record companies were started and run by people who either were musicians themselves or dedicated, passionate fans, who happened to have a little business savvy.

They were in it for the music.

And that's what the job was when I started at Columbia in 1963.

But sometime in, maybe, the early 70s, the several entertainment conglomerates that held record companies within their portfolios, took a look at those comparatively small operations and came to the stunning realization that these little record companies were making money.

So, watch out. Here comes "Corporate"!

And little-by-little, those record execs who were in it for the music were replaced by "suits" who were in it for the $$$.

And that brought about a new job position that lazily stole that old job title: "A&R".

(You'd think they could've come up with a new name – like "no talent bloodsuckers".)

But anyway these new "A&R" people were guys hired to protect the company's investment. They didn't have any ability to be record producers but they were called "A&R" and it seemed to me they were not helping records get made but, instead, we're <u>getting in the way</u>.

Now suddenly we actual record producers had to satisfy some guy in polyester who used phrases like "bottom-line", "marketing strategy" and "target audience"—implying the irrelevance of our criteria like Soulful Performance, Fresh Approach, Virtuosity, Beauty and Art.

(The perceptive reader will note my seething ill temper about corporate casual debasement and lack of respect for an exacting profession. Perhaps the term, "no talent bloodsuckers" is a clue.)

TRACK 54 — D.S.

After a year or so of music lessons, you learn that the letters, D.S., stand for "del segno", Italian words directing you to return to an earlier section of the piece.

In 2016 I got a D.S.

It was actually in the form of a Facebook message from New Zealand noting that November 25 would mark the 40th anniversary of The Last Waltz and inviting me to be the Honorary Musical Director for a series of concerts that would re-create that event.

> But ... what???
> New Zealand???
> Was this the pipe-dream of some stoner lying on a couch thinking through a cloud of smoke, "Wouldn't it be cool if ...?"

Nope.

Following through, I got a reply from a legitimate production company called "Liberty Stage", essentially a one-woman operation run by Simone Williams, the sanest, most pleasant concert producer I'd ever hope to meet.

Spurred on by her husband, Murray's love of the Last Waltz movie and recording, she'd found enough corroborating enthusiasm to book a 3-city tour of Auckland, Christchurch and Wellington in magnificent theaters reminiscent of the splendor of the original Winterland show.

I still wasn't convinced. It's a long trip to New Zealand. There were closer places I wanted to visit. I hadn't even been to Coney Island yet, for goodness sake!

But my mind was changed when Simone sent me a video of a rehearsal and YouTube links to the artists who would participate.

These guys were great! Their musicianship and dedication to the songs was first-rate. This could be fun and something to be proud of.

Garth and his wife, Sister Maud, were to come along too along with a pair of their youthful helpers. And my manager, Andrew, would be there to help with any business that came up.

So off we went.

At the first rehearsal I realized immediately how good the musicians were.

And, on top of that, at one point C.C. commented. "Look! No egos. No back-biting. We're not in America anymore."

For each show Garth played long, intros to "Chest Fever" and "The Weight".

Reflecting during those long, long, long, long intros, I was aware of how transparent they were. Maybe it's because I knew Garth better than most of the people there but I could tell from his ramblings over the keyboard what kind of mood he was in.

One night he would be troubled and he'd have to work through a series of dissonant chords until he lifted himself out of it with passages of the hymns he was so familiar with. Other times, his mood would be buoyant and his playing was capricious, teasing and just plain joyous.

We closed each show with the audience singing along to the chorus of "I Shall Be Released", followed by a couple of encores and that would be it.

They were terrific shows.

L-R: Maud, Garth, Reb Fountain, Mike Hall, Brett Adams, Dave Khan, Adam McGrath, Tami Neilson, Barry Saunders, Delaney Davidson

For my part I was able to move things along efficiently in the right direction.

And, as opposed to the brusqueness of the twenty-something Musical Director in 1976, I had acquired some grace and consideration for others' feelings. That was a real good thing.

A composer will put a D.S. in a piece because she or he figures that a section of the music deserves to be heard again.

I didn't think there was anything particular about the Last Waltz that I needed to experience again.

But once again I was surprised.

All my professional life as a record producer, I've had to fight the frustration of working on other people's material when I could be working on my own.

But I realized in the course of this New Zealand project that I had considerable value as a Facilitator, an Expeditor, a Director.

It had taken me 40 years to come to peace with that.

CODA

The Food Of Love
Leonard Bernstein wrote a popular book in 1959 called "The Joy of Music".

Shakespeare's Duke Orsino in "Twelfth Night" had seen the joy in it: *"If music be the food of love ... Play on!"*

If Orsino found joy in <u>hearing</u> it, does it follow then that there must be an even greater joy in <u>making</u> it?

> With all of us, music and joy are twinned up. Sometimes we're so happy we can't help but whistle or sing to ourselves.

> It sure makes me happy. I've always been in this for the music.

I love music – for what music itself is, not particular performances or artists or compositions – just music itself.

Like the simple relationship of notes to each other.

> For instance, two guitar chords in a bossa nova song may be exactly the same except that one note is different, one finger moving up or down one fret.
> A minimal change. But, as far as the mood and the possible emotions evoked by this subtle change, <u>whole new worlds</u> open up.
> In the simplest terms, it might be major to minor.

318

That to me is a natural wonder.

And then there's rhythm: where those notes fall in the matrix of time. Math.

"Music is nothing but unconscious arithmetic."
(Gottfried Wilhelm Leibniz)

Well, Leibniz got that right. It's not complicated math. Not like the sines and co-sines of trigonometry that baffled me in high school. Music is the most beautiful, the simplest of Living Math.

When I first started making music with someone else – duets at first, then school marching bands, then the bands I formed with other kids – right away we felt the math in it.

We had to adhere to a regular tempo. We had to cooperate, stay "in the pocket".

And that's a special kind of joy, playing with others. It promotes human kinship. It crosses age differences, gender differences, racial differences, cultural differences. It's a big Musical Pie and we're all eating it together.

Speaking of people making music together, here's a great true story:

"Pop" Stoneman was one of country music's first successful artists. According to the internet, he and Hattie had 23 children. (Twenty-three!! That could accurately be called "a passel") Anyway, Pop got the surviving progeny to all play in an act called The Stoneman Family.

Taj told me this tale: when someone asked Pop how he got all his kids to play he said, "Wull, ah bought mahself a fiddle an' a gittar an' a mandolin an' a banjo an' ah laid 'em out theyah on mah bed an' ah said t'mah kids, 'Don't you touch them instruments!'"

* * *

Q & A:

Sometimes I get the question: "When you were making (fill in name of record here), did you know it would be a hit?"

A simple question deserves a simple answer.

No.

Sometimes people ask, "Have you heard this or that new artist?" and I almost never have. There's nothing new under the sun. And, since I'm no longer a Young Turk eager to be up-to-speed on what's popular, I'm not interested enough in trends to want to listen to something other than the music I've always appreciated.

I get sent samples from bands who want to work with me cuz their music is reminiscent of The Band.
Well, that may be true but that's not enough. There already was a The Band.

Another question I get: "Are you proud of the work you've done?"

That's a trickier question.

Proud of <u>what</u> work? I don't think what the questioners imagine as the work I've done is actually the work I've done.

Here's what I think I've done:

I functioned pretty much the same with The Band, Leonard, Janis, BS&T, Lightfoot, and Mama Cass as with Den Dinkwad: take the raw materials and make a record out of them.

And ultimately, I was the one responsible to the record company to deliver an album. So I kept that in the back of my mind while letting it happen. If the train got too far off the track, I'd coax it back on.

I'm proud that I was able to do that.

I'm always happy when, in addition to keeping the train on the track, I have some <u>creative</u> input in the project. Arranging, playing, conducting.

I'm proud of the arrangements I did for artists, whether they were ideas for rhythm patterns or parts for strings or horns.

I've used Michael Franks' "Underneath The Appletree" as a showpiece for horn writing and any of Gordon Lightfoot's string arrangements too.

I'm really proud of the songs I've written for my own albums too, although that question, "How do we categorize them?" always comes up. In record stores, I've seen my albums in the same alphabetized "rock" section as "The Screaming Death Mummies" and wondered.

So, yes, overall I'm proud of what I've done. And, in the end, I'm really, really grateful for how things are turning out.

How <u>did</u> it all turn out?

"You can take all the water, but you can't dry up the fountain."

My creative fountain simply won't dry up. There's music and language floating around in my brain constantly and sometimes I feel like writing it down.

These days I have a regular piano-playing gig on Thursday nights fronting a jazz trio at the classiest restaurant in our little town.

I'm extremely grateful for the opportunity to play weekly and keep my "chops" up – I call it my "jazz gym". I've become a better piano-player.

People come up and compliment the band. And then someone will stop and remark, "Hey, you used to BE somebody." Or words to that effect.

Last year I got a call telling me that my alma mater, Norwalk High School wanted to induct me into their Wall of Fame. They really didn't have a <u>Hall</u> of Fame to set aside, the high school halls generally being full of kids between classes, but they did have a Wall.

I had met the great pianist/composer Horace Silver at a Grammy event some years earlier. He, also a graduate of Norwalk High School, told me that, in spite of having been voted The Best This-or-That in numerous jazz polls, his election to "The Wall" was one of the most meaningful honors he'd received.

There's something about succeeding in the eyes of your home-town crowd.

Last Chords

Writing these pages and vacuuming the hard drive of my memory to recall what it felt like to be that person back then, I've felt a surprising separation between my selves, then and now. It's been a real interesting exercise, at times revealing and at other times cloudy.

As my friend, Paul Gorman has quipped, the subtitle of any autobiography should be "Who I Thought I Was Then By Who I Think I Am Now".

TRUTH, LIES & HEARSAY

TRUTH, LIES OR HEARSAY?

So now I've written all this down, read it, changed it, read it and changed it again, tinkered with it some more. And now I'm ready to get it off my desktop.

It's got some Truth, some Lies (noted as such where they occur) and a pretty big dose of Hearsay.

Truth?

I've shown drafts to a few people and, whether or not they liked it, they all commented that (except for the technical jargon I filched from others) they could really hear my voice coming off the pages.

So that's good and covers the Truth component in the book's title.

Lies?

I've always held accomplished musicians, jazz or otherwise, in such high esteem that I've longed to be on a par with the very best of them.

My position has allowed me to hire the Illustrious Ones for recording sessions and to play alongside them. It feels like some of their Magic Dust rubs off on me. I can hold my own in their company but it wouldn't be truthful to assume that that's enough to put me in their league.

(Note to my meager but appreciative following: you who make up my modest coterie of supporters are meager only in total numbers. Each of you is a giant in your generous appreciation and I extend a deep, heart-felt thank-you to each of you for your support and warmth.)

Hearsay?

323

Well, everybody likes a good story. And the better it is, the more eager we are to move it from Hearsay into Truth. So I'm not always sure where to draw the line. But, if it brings some wonder or a smile and doesn't hurt anyone, well, fine.

* * *

There's an old Zen joke that has a vaguely spiritual ring to it and can close the book on this book:

"There is no right. There is no wrong. Am I right?"

wrong?   right?

THE END

DISCOGRAPHY, ETC.

(during the years for which no entries appear, I was just writing, performing, playing and living.)

1963–1965 : Apprenticeship at Columbia Records
    Original Cast albums. Producer: Goddard Lieberson
    Legacy Series. Producer: Goddard Lieberson
    The Badmen, The Irish Rebellion, Doctors, Drugs & Diseases,
    Mexico

1965–1966: first productions at Columbia
    Point Of Order, The Army/McCarthy Hearings
    Kenyon Hopkins: The Reporter (TV soundtrack)
    Frankie Yankovic (2 albums)
    Skitch Henderson and The Tonight Show band
    Woodstock (Maryland!!) Jesuit Singers
    Charles Lloyd: "Of Course, Of Course"
    The Cyrkle (2 albums)
    The Medium Is The Massage. Marshall McLuhan
    Ten Tuff Guitars
    The Baroque Inevitable
    Brute Force: "Confections Of Love"
    Simon & Garfunkel: "Bookends"
    Leonard Cohen's 1st album

1966:   as an independent producer/arranger
    Blood, Sweat & Tears: 1st album

JOHN SIMON

1967:   'You Are What You Eat' (movie soundtrack)
        Gordon Lightfoot: "Did She Mention My Name"

1968:   The Band: "Music From Big Pink"
        Big Brother & The Holding Company: "Cheap Thrills"
        The Electric Flag: 2nd album
        Mama Cass: solo album
        "Last Summer", soundtrack
1969:   The Band: 2nd album ("the brown album")

1970:   "John Simon's Album"
        Seals & Crofts: "Down Home"
        Touring with Taj Mahal

1971:   Jackie Lomax
        Touring with Taj

1972:   Bobby Charles
        John Hartford: "Morning Bugle"
        My 2nd album: "Journey"
        The Staton Brothers
        The Ducks

1973:   Cyrus Faryar
        Sapo

1974:   Rachel Faro
        Randy Handley

1975:   Rachel's 2nd album
        The Cate Brothers

1976:   Al Kooper solo
        Galdston & Thom
        Hirth Martinez: "Big, Bright Street"

"The Last Waltz"

1977: Gil Evans: "Priestess"
       Dave Sanborn: "Heart To Heart"
       Elizabeth Barraclough
       The Lunsfords

1978: "Soundstage" with Proctor & Bergman
       "Best Little Whorehouse In Texas", original cast album
       Matrix (2 albums)
       Gary McMahan

1979: Michael Franks: "Tiger In The Rain"
       Steve Forbert: "Jackrabbit Slim"
       Twyla Tharp at BAM

1980: Twyla on Broadway

1981: Oratorio: "Rehearsal For Utopia"
       "Imaginary Invalid"

1982: Bireli LaGrene
       "Rock & Roll: The First 5000 Years"

1984: "The Comedy Zone"
       "Accentuate The Positive": The Songs of Johnny Mercer
       Playing piano in a bar in New Jersey

1985: "Archie & Veronica" musical

1987: "Billionaire Embryos", musical

1989: Futu Futu
       "Our Common Future", Lincoln Center
       "Alone Together For The First Time Again"

JOHN SIMON

1990: Pierce Turner

1991: "Out On The Street"

1992: The Band Re-constituted
1st Japan tour

1993: A.J.Croce
Kip's Bay Coeli Band

1994: Jackie Cain & Roy Kral: "Forever"
Lainie Kazan

1995: "Harmony Farm"

1996: Keiko Lee

1997: Motoharu Sano
Jason White

1998: "Home"

1999: Hirth: "I'm Not Like I Was Before"

2000: "Hoagyland"

2002: Toku

2005: "No Band"
First of regular Thursday night jazz trio gigs

2006: Taj gigs

2011: premiere of "Jackass Flats"

2012:   first "rock talk"

2014:   Forbert

2016:   "Last Waltz New Zealand"

2017:   finished "The Amazing Sunshine Traveling Medicine Show"

2018:   Finished this book.

GRATITUDE LIST:

U nder my name on the title page, it should read "with a lot of help from C. C. Loveheart." Almost all the writing in this book is mine but, with her wit and insights, my dear Life Partner and legally-wed spouse, C.C. gave so generously of her time, sensitivity, love, acumen and humor that she deserves to be given credit and thanks.

Coming up with funny lines is as effortless for her as breathing. This book you're reading ran through her "filter" so, when something in here brings you a smile, chances are you have her to thank. (She didn't write that last sentence.)

Andrew Genger, my sort-of-manager is the most ardent Music Fan I know. It was he who first urged me to corral the endless stories I would tell him in answer to his youthful desire to know "what it was really like."

My daughter, Sophie Oberstein, read various sections of the manuscript and offered her intelligent observations.

When it came to editing, Ann Poe, an actual professional literary editor, did just that.
Howard Bilerman, when he found out that this was a book-in-progress, contacted the stellar writer, Greil Marcus, who recommended me to top-flight literary agent, Paul Bresnick, who lifted my spirits to the sky when he told me he loved the manuscript and proudly carried it from cyber-door to cyber-door seeking a publisher.

Jessie Hughes from Amazon's White Glove imprint was genially patient waiting for my re-writes.

Woodstock pal, John Sebastian, in all honesty told me he liked the first half of the book better than the last.

My friend, George Gilbert, as always, was someone I could go to for caring legal wisdom and experience.

And Manny Moreira bludgeoned me to heed the advice of C.C. and others who had read the manuscript and said, "Make it more personal!"

In addition, these others, family and friends, also read portions of the book and offered their insights:

Gregory Stall, Bob Grossman, Max Gregan, Sienna Gregan, Tom McAffrey, Lee Gabites, Michael and Mary Ann Cinellli, Steve Israel, Frank Platt, Jared Levine, Daniel Rorer

And, in addition, my gratitude goes out to those who contributed with reminiscences, photos, etc:

Tanya Snider, Tom Tierney, Sally Grossman, Elliott Landy, Phil Weinstein, Kevin Yatarola, Linda Cypert, et al

And to everyone who appears in this memoir and has, obviously, made a lasting impression in My Musical Life So Far, I couldn't have done this without you.

(With apologies to all those wondrous people whose omission has been dictated by limitations of time, space and the swiss cheese of my memory.)

Sincere and diligent efforts have been made to secure permissions for the use of the photographs appearing in this memoir.

As of the date of publication, gratis permission has been granted for photos from Sony Music Corp, rock photographer Elliott Landy and several private collections.

If subsequently, other rights holders should wish to withhold their permission for the use of their photos, those images will be eliminated from future printings of this book and other images substituted in their place.

***